The Concierge LIFE

KELLYANN SCHAEFER

CONCIERGE PRESS
Newtown, Pennsylvania

Concierge Press
PO Box 753
Newtown PA 18940

ISBN-10:XXXXXXXX
ISBN-13: XXXXXXXX

Editor: Bryna René Haynes, TheHeartofWriting.com
Cover design: Marianna Zotos
Cover photography: Brenda Jankowski, BrenPhotography.com
Interior layout and design: Bryna René Haynes, TheHeartofWriting.com

The Concierge Academy™ is a trademark of Kellyann Schaefer.

Th s book is dedicated to my husband and four
children, who provide me with unconditional
love and support. Without you, this
entrepreneurial journey would
not be possible

Praise

FOR THIS BOOK

"*The Concierge Life* is a labor of love written from Kelly's actual, practical experience. Kelly's thoughtful and oftentimes witty narrative is a book you will refer back to often. *The Concierge Life* will inspire you to keep moving forward, provide encouragement for the tough days and offers an instant advantage for building a successful concierge company of your own!"

- LESLIE SPOOR, CCS, President, Concierge Business Solutions®;
Business Consultant, Concierge Software, Trainer, Mentor

"I believe that, beyond Kelly's ability to write a great book and build a great business, she is also a mind reader! So many things she has written are true to my journey in the concierge world, and reflect the stories of my concierge friends. This book is an inspiration for *every* concierge business owner to reflect, refine their plans for success, and start building their dream."

- SUE GLEW, Best Friend Errand Service

PRAISE FOR KELLYANN SCHAEFER & THE CONCIERGE ACADEMY

"There is no other place to go than the Concierge Academy if you want to grow a successful personal concierge business. The lessons taught here are tried and true and, if put into practice consistently, will have you well on your way to running a successful business. Thank you so much Kelly, for everything you've taught me thus far. You are the model to follow if you want to know what success in this industry looks like."

- WILLIAM BAUMAN, We Got This, LLC

"I have been in business and known Kelly through the ICLMA for about four years. If her course had existed when I began, I would have saved time and money instead of figuring out the process alone. Even now that my business that is growing and has clientele, I find her knowledge and material to be invaluable in filling in the blanks and expanding my business. In summary, I rate her course a 10+!"

- NICOLE CARVER, Carver Concierge, LLC

"Since working with Kelly, I am more confident as a business owner and I am comfortable talking about and charging the prices I want to be paid. I learned who my ideal client is and how to appeal to them better."

- PAVLINA, Boston, Massachusetts

"Thank you, Kelly, for being an inspiration and kicking me in the butt. Since I started working with you, I have signed on thirteen new clients and grown my team from two to six! I am not kidding you! My head is spinning, but I keep pressing on. Thank you!"

- ASHLEY, South Dakota

TABLE *of* CONTENTS

The Concierge LIFE

Introduction

WALK IN MY SHOES

"WHY DID YOU LEAVE NURSING?"

That was the number one question on everyone's mind (and lips!) when they heard I had started a concierge business. And I admit, for the first couple of years, that question really bothered me. I think I kinda felt ashamed. I mean, why does one leave a well-respected, established helping profession like registered nursing?

The answer is simple: I wanted something more. I had a *longing* for something more. I had a longing to do the one thing that gives me more joy than pretty much anything else (besides dancing), and that is taking care of people.

You see, since the age of four, I've been a "mother hen." I was always hovering over the other kids in the neighborhood: trying to keep them safe, ensuring they didn't run out into the middle of the street, reminding them to get home in time for dinner. I was always the responsible one.

As I grew into adulthood, I became the "go-to" gal. I always wanted to help other people through whatever they were dealing with: life, health, and even simple everyday issues.

In my twenties, I decided to translate this passion for helping others into a career in nursing, which fulfilled my desire to care for people and their families. Th s chapter of my life—working in a healthcare setting—lasted a full twenty-one years. I thoroughly enjoyed my tenure in specialty areas, post-surgical units, and nursing management, but the work took its toll on me.

Nursing, while rewarding in many ways, was starting to eat my soul. I was pouring out help to others, but not getting filled up myself.

Time passed. My family grew bigger and bigger. In the midst of this, I was working twelve-hour shifts (which always turned into fifteen-hour shifts). My husband was also working 120 hours a week.

Burnout was rampant, in healthcare and in my home. Its effects spilled over into every area of my life. I needed a change if my soul was to survive. And my heart was nudging me to make an even bigger difference in the world. I knew there something more out there waiting for me.

Clinging to sanity in the middle of this chaos, I took

notice of a seemingly simple thing: every day, patients were being sent home from the hospital all by themselves, with no one to take care of them. For some, even little things, like changing their beloved kitty's litter box, would now become impossible tasks—tasks with no one to complete them.

In that moment, my soul pulled me forward into an amazing opportunity to take care of people on *my* terms, in whatever way they needed most. I no longer wanted to be the one signing discharge papers. I wanted to be the one who saw to those tasks that needed doing afterward. I wanted to be able to solve problems for people, not just in healthcare, but in life.

That's how my company, Task Complete, was born. I'll be honest: I carried a lot of fear around leaving my job and starting a new journey as a business owner. But under the fear was a growing glimmer of hope and excitement, and it propelled me slowly forward. If I went through with this, I could take all the love I had to give and spread it around in a bigger way throughout my community. And so, with butterflies in my belly and terror in my head, I took a deep breath and leapt into my new concierge business.

Having the ability to completely alleviate someone's pain is an amazing feeling. Task Complete has helped single dads have meals with their children, busy CEO moms have food in the house and lunches packed in the morning, and elders take care of kitty's litter and other vital household chores when they're fresh out of the hospital. My team and I routinely create calm out of chaos. My work is creative and complex, and always brings something interesting and different. Every day I find a new challenge to conquer.

Most of all, I know that I would never be able to take care of as many people in a day as a nurse as I do now as a concierge.

There are people in this world who were just born to take care of others. I'm one of those people, and I'm guessing you are, too. Like me, you live for that moment when, after you've cleared twenty-eight years of accumulated clutter out of someone's spare bedroom, you get to see their grateful, happy faces, and know that their grandkids have a place to stay for the fi st time in nearly three decades. My successes aren't just *my* successes; they're my clients' victories, too. That is the power of what we do.

Now, I not only help my clients as a personal concierge, I also support others to create their own thriving concierge businesses. It's why I wrote this book, and why I founded The Concierge Academy™. The student has become the teacher, and I've discovered that the coaching side of my business is just as rewarding as direct service.

If you are organized, live for taking care of people, and excel at creating calm out of chaos, you will *love* being a concierge! And, with the right tools and support, you can turn that love into a thriving business.

But, here's the thing: running a concierge business (or any service business) is *not* for the faint of heart. It takes persistence, deliberation, and serious resilience to establish, maintain, and grow your business. It also takes a willingness to invest in yourself.

Sadly, I've witnessed many personal concierge companies close up shop because they didn't understand how their businesses worked, couldn't wrap their heads around effective marketing, or weren't willing to invest the time and money necessary to build relationships.

That's why I'm going to teach you all of that—and more—in this handy little book you're holding.

My business didn't fl p right out of the gate, but it didn't truly launch until I learned the lessons I'm about to share with you in this book. So, get ready, because I'm about to dispel the false beliefs that take down so many fl dgling concierge businesses, and show you *exactly* what to do to grow your business the way I did (while avoiding the pitfalls no one warned me about).

Lesson one: Be willing to learn and try new things! With that in mind, let's get started, so you can get out there and start changing lives!

With love,

Chapter 1

WHAT IT *REALLY* MEANS TO BE A PERSONAL CONCIERGE

BEING IN THE SERVICE BUSINESS as a professional concierge is *awwwwesome*! It allows me to integrate my organization, communication, and productivity skills with my love of taking care of people. And as my business continues to grow, I get to impact even more lives because I've also been able to gather an amazing, cohesive team. With a variety of unique skills and talents, we come together to help our clients tackle all of the items on their to-do lists, which in turn improves their overall quality of life—a goal every concierge shares.

I am *so* blessed. The one thing I love to do above all things—taking care of people—has become more than my livelihood. It's become my way of life.

Down to my core, I love people, and I love life! I love how people are the same, and I love how they are different. I love their stories. I love being able to come up with an action plan for them in under ten minutes because I know people so well. This is my gift in life, and my concierge business is how I get to share it with the world. (Since you're reading this book, I'm pretty sure that you have a gift you want to share, too!)

Things weren't always rainbows and unicorns for me, though. Building my concierge business took time and perseverance. Many people make the mistake of thinking that being a concierge is going to be easy—but it's still a business, no matter how fun it is, and building a business takes commitment and hard work. (More on that later.) I created my success through a sometimes-grueling series of trials and errors, changes and modifications. You might even say I took the "scenic route!"

Luckily, you don't have to walk that same scenic path to get to where you want to be.

What I'm going to teach you in this book isn't a shortcut, because there are no shortcuts to real success. But I am going to put you on the path, and share my journey so that you can tackle that path with comfy shoes and a state-of-the-art GPS!

Let's continue, shall we?

THE FOUNDATION
of a SUCCESSFUL
CONCIERGE BUSINESS

Tell me if this story sounds familiar to you …

When I first started my business, I was doing everything I could think of to get clients, but things weren't happening fast enough.

Everyone I spoke to loved the concept of my business. At every networking event I went to, people would say, "Oh, you must be so busy! Everyone needs what you do!" I would put on a smile, nod, and say, "Yes, very busy."

On the inside, though, I was embarrassed. I felt like an utter failure. If these people found out that I only had a few clients, they would think I was a phony and likely wouldn't hire me! Sadly, the shame and fear of being "not good enough" kept me running in circles for the first two years of my business. I was always comparing, self-criticizing, and tearing myself down.

But this shame also fueled me, because I knew how deeply I wanted to make this business work. I had a mission to take care of others, and I refused to stop until I successfully created a business that would serve as many people as possible in my local community. (My big vision now blows away the vision I had for myself back then—but I'll save that story for later.)

After trying and failing to "get it right," I was on the verge of giving up; instead, I decided to work with a business coach. My results were only so-so and I became even more deflated. "Is this ever gonna work?" I wondered. Then, I found another business coach, and then another. I wanted someone to give me all the right answers to help me keep my business afloat. The coaches I connected with were all good people, but none of them could address the unique struggles and challenges I faced as a concierge. They didn't fully understand my business. Some of their strategies worked a little, and some… well, not so much. Still, even the few nuggets I learned from these mentors ultimately changed the way I do business. I still didn't have a shortcut to success, but I decided that if I took everything that worked even a little, I could adapt and amplify it.

For the next two years, I tracked every new client, honed in on my ideal client, and became very clear about what I do and how I really impact our clients' lives. I tracked what worked, and what didn't. By reviewing the information and statistics I collected, I was able to identify very specific actions and strategies within my marketing that were really working. Once I did this, I could easily repeat these strategies, feeling confide t that they would bring me even more of the right clients—which then allowed me to do more of the one thing I am destined to do: take care of people.

I formulated a clear plan. I hustled. I fumbled. I fell down more times than I can count. But I always came back to my goals, course-corrected, and got back on the journey. That's what having a "mission" will do to you!

Yes, reviewing all of my successes and mistakes revealed an actual method to my madness! I found specific actions I could do over and over again that created results every single time I implemented them. That's when things started to really take off.

I made giant strides that year. Not everyone takes time to map out a strategy, but—as I discovered—it's key when you're running a concierge business (or any business, for that matter) to have a plan—a business GPS. Without a map, not only can you not see where your path is headed, you're leaving it to chance whether you'll reach your destination at all.

I have a secret to share: *you can absolutely do this in your business, too.* You just need to get a handle on the basics, concentrate on what works for you and your clients, and put in the work to get things rolling. Momentum doesn't just happen; we must create it. An overall plan of right actions, done consistently, is the best and surest way to create big results!

THE 8 PILLARS OF A SOLID CONCIERGE BUSINESS

When I first started Task Complete, I had *zero* business knowledge other than what I had picked up from books and journals. I read everything I could get my hands on, but implementing that knowledge seemed complicated and time-consuming, and felt like a huge roadblock for me.

Perhaps you've had this happen, too? The concepts and strategies seem solid when you read about them, but when it comes to applying them in real life and actually doing the work of marketing, you have no idea where to begin. All of a sudden, everything seems so *hard*.

It doesn't have to be that way.

Let me introduce the foundation of my business plan, the *8 Pillars of a Solid Concierge Business*. These are the eight most important places to put your time and attention in order to generate buzz, get clients, start making a profit, and truly live the Concierge Life!

You'll notice that there's a theme to this list—and there's a reason for that. There's more to your concierge business than just selling services. Your business is built on the foundation of *relationships!*

Nurture your relationships—in multiple ways, and across multiple platforms—and you *will* grow your business. Everything you will ever do starts with relationships. Th s is the single most important thing to know about being a concierge.

In this book, I'll show you how to tackle each of these items in depth, in exactly the ways that helped me take my business from zero to six figures in just a few years.

The 8 Pillars of a Solid Concierge Business

1. Network, network, network!
2. Build connections
3. Nurture your relationships
4. Stay in touch
5. Educate the marketplace
6. Develop a repeatable, consistent marketing plan
7. Create effective packages
8. Deliver impeccable service

Notice that networking is Step #1. As I struggled to find clients in the first few months of my Concierge Life, I wanted to crawl in a hole and hide. I was a brand new business owner, and I was so nervous.

If you've ever heard me talk about networking, you probably know my story about the very first time I went to a structured networking event. It was a dual local Chamber of Commerce event. Armed with a stack of business cards, I parked my mom van, got out of the car... and hurled, right there under the spotlight in the parking lot. No joke! The fear of walking into a room full of other business owners consumed me in that moment.

I mustered enough strength that night to go inside anyway. I was there to "get business," after all. After mingling nervously for two hours, sharing business cards and telling my stories, I left empty handed. No new clients. I was very deflated. (I had mistakenly thought that cold networking was how you got business.)

After that experience, I wanted nothing more than to hide out in my home office and never show my face at a networking event again. But I knew that wasn't going to help me grow the business I wanted—so instead, I put myself out there, day after day. I made sure I was visible everywhere my ideal clients went.

This helped me accomplish Step #2: build connections quickly. I made myself the face of my business. I wasn't just a nice website (honestly, my web site was homemade and didn't work at the time), or a social media page. I was a *real human being* who was passionate about her business and mission. More importantly, I was a person who listened to people's struggles, and cared deeply enough to help.

As I met new people, I stayed in contact by making and taking phone calls, sending e-mails, and responding to posts on social media—and I never forgot the power of a handwritten note. Nurturing relationships and staying in touch with prospects and contacts became a natural extension of the networking I was doing.

This—the building of strong relationships—was the part that seemed to be missing from all those "marketing" books I had read.

This type of relationship nurturing builds trust and keeps you in the forefront of people's minds. When you show up to connect and not necessarily sell (more on that later), people are open to learning more about you and what you do. Candid conversations help you step into the space where allies, colleagues, and referral partners are born. I'm sure you're aware that people do business with those they "know, like, and trust;" this is a sure-fire way to create that level of relationship with people.

Step #4, stay in touch, is where many concierge business owners fall off the wagon. They know they're supposed to network, but they make the critical mistake of expecting a sale after the first point of contact. As a concierge, you're asking people to invite you into their lives, and maybe even into their homes. That takes a level of trust that goes above and beyond what's required for your average product or service So, as I jokingly remind my Concierge Academy students, never try to get to third base on your first date! Don't go in for the win right away; it's not appealing. Instead, connect, nurture, and create relationships before you attempt to make a sale. Remember to always come from a place of service, not from a place of need or desperation.

The "getting to know you" phase is a great time to educate your contacts on ways to use your services—and, more importantly, how they can *refer business to you.* You can offer value and share your expertise in the way of blogs, articles, and social media. Through trial and error, I discovered how to reach my audience, and speak to them in a way that enabled them to understand how Task Complete would support their lives. The more sure of myself and my message I became, the more people understood the value of what I was offering.

A typical pitfall for many entrepreneurs (both newbies and old hands) is they don't remain consistent. They say, "I tried that once, and it didn't work, so I stopped doing it." In other words, they give up before the strategy they've implemented has a chance to work. That's why I created a system around my marketing that is repeatable and consistent. Systems and repetition create consistency and help you streamline your business. They also increase your confidence, which gives a boost to all of your networking efforts and creates even better, more consistent results.

Consistent action leads to results. Results boost your confidence, which makes you feel great about taking more (consistent) action!

On the flip side, when you don't have the right systems and strategies in place, you'll eventually feel defeated and deflated, or like you're flailing in the dark. When things don't work out the way you were hoping, or don't happen fast enough, your frustration may lead you to doubt whether starting a business was a good idea at all.

I've watched too many concierges walk away from their dreams because they weren't consistent in their marketing for long enough. Believe me, you don't want to get to that point! The whole reason you became a concierge in the first place was to create effective packages that serve people, and deliver impeccable service to everyone who needs your help. Giving up because of a few simple mistakes—like not marketing effectively, or not creating systems for relationship nurturing—would be a tragedy.

You have so much to share, and so many people to help. If you focus on and implement my 8 Pillars of a Solid Concierge Business, as well as what you learn in the rest of this book, you'll start to see positive results sooner than you think!

WHAT IT TAKES *to* CREATE THE CONCIERGE LIFE

While many of us are born to take care of people, not everyone is a natural entrepreneur. Most of us need some fine tuning, guidance, and support. The entrepreneurial world can be harsh at times, and super lonely.[1]

How do you know if you have what it takes? Let's take a look at your skill set.

Some of the core qualities that make a great concierge are:

- Natural organization and self-motivation.

- The ability to problem solve.

- Being that "go-to" person.

- A burning desire to help others.

- Passion for a business that not only serves clients, but fills you up in the process.

(1) Connect with other concierges at Facebook.com/groups/ConciergeConnections

In addition to these often-inborn qualities, though, you also need to become a prolific   marketer!

What you need most when starting out in the concierge business:

- A solid business foundation.

- An influx of clients (and cash), fast.

- A way to identify and connect with your ideal clients.

- Packages and pricing that compel people to say "yes!"

- A structured intake process.

- A reputable and effective online presence.

- Focus and discipline. (You have to be willing to get out there over and over again!)

- And, most importantly, a kickass marketing plan—because you can't make a difference if no one knows you're out there!

As you can see, having the skills to be a great concierge isn't enough. You have to learn to be a smart business-person, too.

Not taking their marketing and business strategies seriously is the *#1 biggest mistake* most concierge business owners make, and the biggest reason why so many concierge businesses fail in the first few years. Many want to do this amazing work, but they don't invest the time, attention, and resources needed to get out of the starting gate and get visible in the marketplace.

It's unsettling (to say the least) when your passion and dreams hit smack up against fear, bewilderment, and loads of unanswered questions. I know, because it happened to me! In 2010, when I started Task Complete, there were no resources to guide me through the process of building a successful concierge business, and no single resource I could turn to for help. There were lots of books that gave me bulleted lists of things to do, but they all lacked real-life strategies and conversations about what it takes to create a successful Concierge Life. I had to invest multiple five figures in coaches, programs, and business books to get all the pieces I needed to create my success strategies.

The lack of resources out there for people like us is exactly what led me to write this book, and to create The Concierge Academy™. It's my solution to the problems, pitfalls, and frustrations of growing a concierge business on your own without support. I believe, deep within my core, that not everyone was born to take care of other people. But if it's your burning desire to do this work, you have that gift— nd I'm going to give you what you need to succeed.

As you'll see in this book, I'm a straight shooter, and I don't sugarcoat reality. I tell it like it is—the good, the bad, and the ugly—because I want every motivated, talented concierge in my world to build a profitable business and become an industry leader, *without* having to go through the same struggles I did.

I know my strategies work because I've taken my business from an army of one—me!—to a thriving, multi-six-figure enterprise with a team of eight gorgeous souls *in under four years.* I want *you* to thrive in the same way.

I don't know about you, but when I started my business, I wanted more than just a job. I wanted to build a legacy. My ultimate goal is to positively impact a million lives. (Remember when, a couple of pages back, I mentioned how my goal now is so much bigger than the one I started with? Yeah, baby!) That's why I'm so passionate about sharing my success secrets with you. There is nothing I want more than to help you create your very own awesome-sauce Concierge Life.

So, are you ready to join me?

Let's do this!

Chapter 2

THE 6 FALSE BELIEFS THAT WILL CRUSH YOUR DREAMS (AND MAYBE YOUR BUSINESS, TOO)

A FEW YEARS AFTER I started my business, I sat down to take a "personal inventory." I was curious not only about how far I'd come, but what my biggest mistakes were. Now, before we go any further, I want to say that I don't actually believe in mistakes, because any "mistake" is just a learning opportunity in disguise, and what you do with those learning opportunities decides your future outcomes. However, when I took my inventory, I could see that there were definately things I had done that took me the long way around. Even more, there were *beliefs* I carried around my business and my progress that made my first years in business more challenging, physically, financially, and mentally.

Sitting alone at my desk, I opened my journal and started writing down my thoughts about my concierge business, and the bumps I've hit along the way, like:

- I thought it was going to be much easier than it was to get clients.

- I thought that, since I like taking care of people (and since everybody told me how much they just *loved* the concept of what I was doing), everyone would be a potential client.

- Based on everything I read in books and online, I thought that I would need very little startup money.

- I thought I didn't need to invest in myself or hire a business coach.

- I thought I could do it all on my own, by myself, because I'm great at what I do.

When I put my pen down and reread what I'd written, I sat there and thought long and hard about what I had been through. How much time had I wasted, and how many detours had I taken, because my beliefs about what it would take to be successful in this business were so off-base?

And if *I* had made less-than-ideal choices because of these false beliefs, had other people done the same thing? Or was I the only foolish one?

I decided to reach out to several other personal concierges with whom I had built relationships over the past few years, people I had grown with and looked up to. I polled them to ask what they believed their top mistakes were—and I have to admit, I was shocked. They felt they had made the *exact same mistakes* I did!

That's when I truly realized I was on to something. In those days and months after I made my list, I realized that by making those mistakes myself (and feeling so passionate about them) I had an opportunity to help others in our industry avoid those same mistakes! If I could guide others avoid those initial startup traps, I could save people years of struggle as they worked to get their businesses off the ground.

As time went on, more and more people wanted my advice and my support. I started looking for a way to share my story so that concierges like you would know that they are not alone, and that it doesn't have to be an uphill battle. You *can* do what you love and make money at the same time —I'm living proof!

And that, my friend, is exactly why I wrote this book and created The Concierge Academy: to prevent others from making the same mistakes I did. I want to teach you to grow a successful and profitable concierge company, and help you ditch the false beliefs that made my first years in business so rocky.

In the beginning, I didn't price my services properly. I was afraid to invest in myself and my business. I thought everyone was a potential client. And, on top of that, I thought I could figure it all out on my own. *I'm a smart girl,* I thought. *I managed to get through nursing school as a single mom, so this whole business thing should be a piece of cake!*

Then, I would stare at my computer and wonder what the hell to do next.

The worst part is that, the more I tried to put myself out there, the more I heard that dreaded word, "no." Being told "no," or having someone not call me back, felt like a direct hit to my self-confidence. I would sit at my desk and cry, wondering what was wrong with me. Every day, it got harder and harder to face the realities of entrepreneurship.

If this sounds like your life right now, there is nothing wrong with you! You just haven't been given all the right information to set yourself up for success.

If you want to steer clear of the mind traps and get your business on the fast track to success, you need to learn to recognize the false beliefs you're holding about what building a concierge business really takes. If you hold any of these beliefs, or try to run your business as though they're true, I can tell you, you're in for a bumpy ride.

So, here they are: The 6 False Beliefs that Will Crush Your Dreams (and Maybe Your Business, Too).

THE 6 FALSE BELIEFS THAT WILL CRUSH YOUR DREAMS
(and Maybe Your Business, Too)

1. You can start a concierge business with $500 and a smile

2. Everybody you know will be a client

3. You don't have to market a concierge business

4. You don't have to invest in a concierge business

5. You don't have to get support, and can figure it all out on your own

6. You can't charge what your time is worth

Any of these sound familiar? I bet they do! And even if you read those bullets and said, "I don't actually believe those things," chances are, on some level, you do—otherwise you wouldn't have picked up this book!

So, let's start cleaning (mental) house!

FALSE BELIEF #1: YOU CAN START A CONCIERGE BUSINESS WITH $500 AND A SMILE

I know you've read those books—the ones that tell you that all you need to make it in this business are some flyers, a cell phone, and a reliable car to get to your clients' houses? Ooh, that makes me seethe. It's complete and utter *bullshit.*

Whew. Okay, rant over!

The truth is, in the beginning, you're afraid to make costly mistakes because you're not sure what's going to work and what isn't. So, you put your energy into "not spending any money," or try throwing things at the wall to see if they stick …and then get frustrated when those tactics don't work.

A lot of the information out there about marketing—for any business—is stale, outdated, and irrelevant in today's market. It might have been effective thirty years ago (although I doubt it), but these days the idea that you can start *any* business for $500 is completely bogus.

Every business needs capital of some sort. You can use your own money (like funds pulled from investments or savings) or borrowed capital (like a loan from the bank or your rich aunt)—but no matter where your funds come from, you *need* cash to invest in your business.

If you're not willing to put your money where your mouth is, you probably won't succeed in business. Why? Because if *you* don't believe enough in what you're doing to invest in it, why should your clients?

(That's a harsh one right there!)

Now, the question of *how much* money you actually need is a bit more complicated. I can't give you a firm number, because I don't know where you live, what your current network looks like, or who your ideal clients are, or your current living situation.

Some people in this industry start by putting aside six months of living expenses and then hit the ground running hard. Others keep working their "day job" and squeeze in concierge work on evenings or weekends.

Whatever path you choose is your own decision based on what's best for you and your family. But know this for sure: when you're ready to get serious, it will be time to hustle.

So do your research, read the rest of this book, and decide what you really need to invest to put your strongest strategies into play to get clients fast. Then, double it! You'll need money up front for insurance, for business cards, and to start networking so that you can build those all-important relationships. As you begin to create momentum, other things will pop up, such as opportunities to do sponsorships and giveaways. You'll also want to put some cash into growing yourself through education and training programs. All these things take money—but don't look at these expenses as "spending." Instead, see them as investments into your Concierge Life.

The lesson here: starting your business won't take millions—but I can guarantee you'll need more than just five hundred bucks and a smile.

FALSE BELIEF #2: EVERYBODY YOU KNOW WILL BE A CLIENT

When I started my business, I was so excited to share it. I knew I had a great concept; after all, *everybody* needs and wants help with daily stuff, right?

Wrong.

Everyone *says* they want help. Not everyone is willing to *pay* for that help.

You see, value is a funny thing. People fantasize about freeing up their time, asking for help, and investing in their own quality of life. But precious few will actually do it—and if you want to succeed as a concierge, you need to hone in on the clients who will make the leap.

I didn't understand this at first. Why was I hearing "no" over and over again? I felt like there was something wrong with me. I could give these people everything they said they wanted—so why weren't they saying "yes"?

Two words, my friend: *Target Market.*

One of the biggest keys to success in this business (and any business) is to identify a clear target market. I made a huge boo-boo when I tried to be a jack of all trades. (Again, I don't believe in mistakes, but this one was definitely a big detour.) By not clearly identifying the people I most wanted to work with, and instead trying to market to everyone, I wasted a lot of time, money, and energy. More, my "everyone is a client" belief diluted my message, which negatively impacted my growth. When *you're* not clear on who you work with and what you do, how can you expect other people to get it?

The worst part was, I kept believing everyone was a client even after I read all the "right" books and invested thousands in training and coaching. "They don't know my business," I told myself. "They can't tell me who to help!" I wanted so desperately to help "everyone" that I spent time and money chasing too many things. I had to learn this lesson over and over again before I finally snapped out of it. Then, once I did, I had to spend *more* money re-branding, re-marketing, and reconnecting with the people who actually wanted what I'd been offering all along.

So, be specific about who you want to serve, and how. Choose just one "target market." You never have to turn down business, but knowing who you're speaking to allows you to address their greatest needs and aspirations in a concise way that helps you navigate ALL your marketing decisions.

FALSE BELIEF #3: YOU DON'T HAVE TO MARKET A CONCIERGE BUSINESS

This one is a direct descendant of False Belief #2, because if you think everyone you know will be a client, why would you spend money on marketing?

Now that you know you can't serve everyone, you need to decide how to reach the people you will serve—and that requires marketing. Not half-assed, inconsistent marketing (like showing up to the occasional networking event and putting up fliers in the grocery story), but real, well-rounded, well-planned—and, most of all, *consistent*—marketing.

We'll talk more about marketing in Chapter 3, but for now I want to make one thing clear: your marketing efforts cannot be like your new fad diet, or your New Year's resolution to go to the gym every day. They can't fizzle out when you get bored of implementing them, or when you get frustrated that they aren't working instantaneously. You need to be consistent in the quality, quantity, and message of every piece of your marketing.

If you want your business to succeed, you've got to get serious about your marketing. Period.

In fact, marketing is going to be the biggest, most time-consuming part of your business. You may spend more time every week on marketing than you do on serving your clients, especially at first—so embrace marketing. Learn to love it.

And just so you know… even after you get clients, you *still* have to market. Marketing will forever be a part of your Concierge Life. In fact, it will become your best friend!

FALSE BELIEF #4: YOU DON'T HAVE TO INVEST IN A CONCIERGE BUSINESS

Growing your concierge business and making it successful in the long term requires more than just that initial (far more than $500) startup cash. It requires investing in your business and in yourself as a business owner.

Th s is one of those funny things about business that I was not prepared for, and still struggle with at times. You may be thinking that, once you get things up and running and get your marketing squared away, you won't have to put any more money into your business. Wrong! In fact, the more you invest in yourself and your business, the more you and your business will grow. Th s is true no matter where you are on your path.

What does investing in yourself and your business look like?

First, it means investing in valuable support from industry experts. Second, it means spending what is needed to make sure you and your brand can show up in a way that meets the expectations of your ideal clients.

When I started out, I networked everywhere. I went to a bunch of women's groups and listened to dozens of people speak. They all talked about getting help, hiring coaches, asking for support, having someone hold your hand and walk you through the steps. In my mind, I was like, "I'm not handing my money over to them!" But after a year of struggling on my own, I finally hired a coach.

As I mentioned in Chapter 1, my first coach didn't provide life-changing results—but I did learn more about myself and what I really wanted to create. I later moved on to another coach, and another, looking for that "perfect advice" that would radically change my business. Again, I gained knowledge from these coaches, but never got the big breakthroughs I was hoping for. I didn't feel like they understood me or the brand I was trying to build. At the same time, I also invested in social media marketing classes, list-building seminars, and client attraction principles. Some things helped me tremendously, other things, not so much.

But even though I hadn't found the magic bullet I wanted, I was slowly gaining traction. In fact, the more time and energy I put into learning, the more my business started to take off. Why? Because I was treating my business like a *business*, not like a hobby.

Eventually, I found an amazing coach who had the skills and tools to guide me along the way. Some of what I learned from her was perfect for this industry, some of it needed to be adjusted to fit. But the real gift of working with her was that, beyond becoming a better business owner, I became a different person—one who said yes to opportunities more freely because I wasn't so afraid.

The greatest part of entrepreneurship is the stuff they never tell you about. It's the way you evolve so that you can show up in the world clear, confident, and committed to your mission. If I had known the value I would find in investing in myself this way, and had known what questions to ask and what to look for, I probably would have found the right coach faster.

The other half of investing in yourself and your business

is remembering that you and your brand are one and the same. Th s means presenting yourself as your brand, and in a way that jives with your ideal clients. That doesn't mean running out to buy a Benz, but it does mean making sure you have what you need to make a good impression.

FALSE BELIEF #5: YOU DON'T HAVE TO GET SUPPORT, AND CAN FIGURE IT ALL ON YOUR OWN

It's funny, we concierges are all about delegation. We want our clients to pass off tasks to us, and trust us to support them in their lives and businesses. But when it comes to our own businesses, we like to think that we don't need the same support—as if we're completely immune.

Personally, I resisted asking for help until I nearly burned myself out. It was okay to go it alone at first, when I was struggling to find clients, but the more successful I became, the busier I got, and the harder I had to work to keep it all rolling.

It's something that we read in all the books, and hear over and over again: get support, get help, delegate, you can't do it all by yourself. But I'm pig-headed, and the books were wrong about so much other stuff that I just said to myself, "You don't know who you're talking to. I balanced four kids and a crazy career. I can handle anything!" And

I did—until I was about to crash, burn, and throw in the towel on everything. I worked so hard that I no longer had my own "balance." I had offically become my ideal client. Trying to push and push not only myself but the business, too … it damn near broke me. (It's a fact that when you push, you only push what you want further away!)

That's when everything shifted for me. So, I swallowed my pride, put on my big girl panties, and did what I needed to do to bring on my first team member to help take care of clients. Why was this so pivotal? Because I no longer had time to market. I was trying to balance clients, marketing, networking, and my own family's needs; something had to give. I had to open up my heart, and my business, and let someone in if I wanted to keep growing.

Once I made the leap, I realized something: delegation is *magic.*

You don't want to be the "bottleneck" in your own business. You can't be the top dog in every arena. If you want to get fast results, you have to ask for help when and where you need it. More, you need to learn from others who are further up the ladder.

Remember when I wrote in Chapter 1 about my "homemade" website? My husband and I sat for hours working on this template thing that was supposed to be "easy." The reality was that I didn't know what I didn't know. Even after all the time and commitment we put into that website, it wasn't the lead generation machine I hoped it would be. It worked well, and it was kinda fun, but it wasn't attracting phone calls (and the primary reason you have a website is to get clients from it, right?).

When I decided to invest a large sum of money into a new website, it was *very* scary. I mean, we're talking about my profit margin for the year! But the designer I hired was an expert, and it took her far less time to build my site the right way than it had taken us to build it the wrong way.

Hiring experts is smart business. Think about them as partners in your success instead of just another place where you're spending money.

The final piece of asking for help is finding (or creating) a community.

Have you ever felt alone as an entrepreneur? You wake up every day and put in eight hours (or more) trying to grow your business, and yet you feel disconnected, and unsure of what to do and where to go. You wish you could talk to someone who's walking the same path, and struggling with the same things. It's even worse if you're like me and don't have friends or family that have ever been brave enough to do this "entrepreneur thing."

The need for community is why I have always belonged to mastermind groups. Some were free, some were paid, but all of them have presented opportunities to meet and connect with people who are exactly at my level and experiencing the same growing pains. In my groups, I can ask questions, learn new strategies, and stay accountable to my goals and dreams. Most of all, I no longer feel like I'm the only one in the world doing what I'm doing!

But, heed this warning: If you become the "smartest" person in the room, it's time to find a new room.

FALSE BELIEF #6: YOU CAN'T CHARGE WHAT YOUR TIME IS WORTH

Aside from not taking their marketing seriously, one of the biggest mistakes new concierges make is that they don't price and package their services properly.

As natural helpers, we tend to undervalue what we offer the marketplace. We want people to be able to afford what we offer, so we discount our services. Please know that your time is just as valuable as anyone else's.

Discounting is actually a big no-no, because your time is your most valuable asset in your business. If you offer your services on the cheap, you'll run out of money fast, especially when you have a team and payroll to cover.

Knowing how to properly gauge your market (and price your services accordingly) is a skill that takes some practice. But here's the thing: when you find the "sweet spot" for your pricing, your ideal clients will bite.

Before I opened my business, I did a price calculation. If I wanted to make X amount of dollars per year (because let's face it, I wasn't starting a business just for the fun of it!),

I discovered that I would have to charge about $80 per hour.

"How is that going to work?" I asked myself. I didn't think the market would bear that price, so I slashed my rates to what I thought would be "acceptable," and set out to recruit my first clients.

The crazy thing was, I had undercut myself, and nobody wanted my services... until I upped my rates. Then, like magic, people were interested; it was as if there was suddenly a greater value attached to what I was offering. Once I learned to market myself effectively and communicate the value of what I was offering, I increased my rates again and got even more clients.

Your rates will depend on a number of factors: your ideal client base, your geographical location, and the nature of your services. But they should always reflect your expertise and the value of the service you're offering.

You *absolutely can* charge what your time is worth. You just have to package it up and sell it right! You'll want to find a rate that feels in alignment with your goals without triggering fears of unworthiness from within. But please remember, your time is just as valuable as your clients' time. Charging $10 an hour may seem like a good idea when you're starting out, but by the time you pay you operating costs, there is little profit left. You'll need to keep this in mind when setting fees.

Most of all, never let anyone else tell you how much you're "worth." That's something that *you* get to decide.

3 THINGS YOU NEED *to* DO RIGHT NOW *to* BOOST YOUR BUSINESS

To me, the secret to success in this arena is to avoid buying into The 6 False Beliefs that Will Crush Your Dreams from the start. If you start out right, you'll keep going that way. And, if you can avoid those traps for the whole beginning stage of your business (two years if you're at it full-time, longer if you're part-time), you will be well on your way to real success.

Now, I don't want to make it sound as though everything I did in my first two years of business was a giant mess. I did a lot of things right, too, and these things laid a strong foundation that kept my business afloat while I took all those other wrong turns.

The top 3 things I did right in my first two years of business:

1. Network
2. Say "Yes" to opportunities
3. Hire a Mentor

So, as you avoid falling victim to the 6 False Beliefs, you also want to make sure you're doing these three things.

#1: NETWORK

Hands down, networking is *the number one way* to get clients. You will not gain clients from behind your computer screen!

(Shocker, I know.)

This is one of the biggest pitfalls for people in *any* industry that provides "personal services." Somehow, many people believe that just putting up a website or sending out a weekly e-mail newsletter will result in clients beating down their doors. But (as you've probably guessed), that is not the case.

As I wrote in Chapter 1, the concierge business is all about relationships. By networking, you are making yourself visible. You're making yourself real to the people you connect with, and you're laying the foundation for real relationships. What we offer is highly personal, so our clients need to know and like us before they write that check.

So, if you're not doing it already, be sure you are out there networking—in person—*at least eight times a month*. No excuses. No exceptions. Just get out there.

#2: SAY "YES" TO OPPORTUNITIES

In the beginning, fear often held me back. I was afraid to say yes to speaking engagements, travel for mastermind groups, or put myself out there as an expert.

Yup. I was comfortable in my comfort zone. But my comfort zone wasn't doing squat to help me grow my business. In fact, every amazing thing that has happened for me in my business was a result of stepping out of my comfort zone and facing my fear.

My advice: say "yes" to every opportunity that moves you toward your goals, even when you're kicking and screaming inside your head, and even when you're not sure how you're going to make it happen. As Richard Branson said, "If someone offers you an amazing opportunity but you are not sure you can do it, say yes—then learn how to do it later!" So…

- If you're asked to speak at the local PTO, or at a Chamber of Commerce networking event, say yes!

- If you have the opportunity to put yourself in front of dozens of your ideal clients, say yes!

- If you're asked to write an article for your local paper or your favorite blog, say yes! (Hint: don't pay for placement. Wait until you're invited.)

If you say yes to every great opportunity that comes your way, you'll only get more great opportunities in the future!

#3: HIRE A MENTOR

As you may have gathered from the rest of this chapter, this was one of the hardest things for me to do in the beginning.

First off, I felt as if I didn't need anyone to teach me anything. I could easily go online and find all the free resources and information in the world to make my business a success. (I was flat wrong.) And second, I had *no* budget to do such a thing!

I quickly realized, though, that to get ahead I needed to be more present, act faster on opportunities, and have someone in my corner cheering me on each step of the way. I needed someone who was a few rungs higher on the ladder, and who could help me cut my learning curve in half. We are social beings: we digest information so much more easily through other people's experiences, whether positive or negative.

When I got to the point where I was a few rungs higher on the ladder, I started my Concierge Academy. I feel like I've come full circle, and now I get to give back. Being on the other side has given me even more of an appreciation for what mentorship can do for new business owners. So if you haven't already done so, consider investing in a coach or mentor who can really guide you through the process of launching and growing your business, and help you learn what it takes for you, personally, to be successful.

The BIG LESSON

I've watched so many people come and go in this industry, and I can tell you, it isn't a lack of skill or desire to succeed that kills their businesses. It's a lack of practical knowledge combined with faulty beliefs about what running a concierge business actually entails. The more you run up against those walls, the more frustrated you will get, and the more your passion and commitment will fizzle.

Now that you know what's real, and what's just a myth, you'll start to gain a whole new perspective on your business, and start making choices that put you on the direct path to success.

You're not alone, and you don't have to do it all on your own. The strategies I'm going to share with you in the rest of this book are powerful, and they *will* work to get you the visibility you need to succeed in this industry.

Your first step is to *fall in love with marketing*.

Chapter 3

GETTING OUT THERE:
THE MARKETING WHEEL

MANY PEOPLE WHO BECOME concierges have the same backstory. They're kind, caring, giving individuals who like helping others and have a gift for GSD (getting shit done). They're able to juggle multiple projects, set timelines, and see where others need a little extra boost.

Concierges are *so* awesome.

(I mean it. You really are awesome!)

But here's the thing that many concierges forget: *being a concierge is not actually your number one job.*

Nope, your number one job as a concierge isn't helping others, although that's a big part of the business.

Your number one job is *marketing*.

Without marketing you'll have no clients. If you have no clients, you have no business. It's a sad truth that I've witnessed many, many times.

It makes my heart sad when I visit a fellow concierge's website and find that it's no longer active. Immediately, I wonder why the business shut down. Was it by choice, or because the business couldn't sustain itself? Was it that the concierge's passion dwindled, or that passion wasn't enough to pay the bills?

This is why the biggest part of what I teach other concierges isn't how to be a great concierge; I'm pretty sure you all can nail that! What I teach is how to be a great marketer so that you can *keep* being a great (and successful) concierge for many years to come.

So, right now, I want you to ask yourself: "How do I really feel about marketing?"

One of my early business coaches told me, "You're going to hear nine no's for every yes."

Good advice, right? But in the first few years in business, I felt like I was hearing a hundred no's for every yes. The reality was, I was talking to the wrong people. I still believed in the myth that says, "Everyone you know is going to be your client." And so every time I got rejected, my confidence took a major hit. It felt horrible.

It took me years to realize that you don't have to hear a hundred no's for every yes *if you talk to the right people.* Not everyone was a potential client—but, more importantly, not everyone was my *ideal* client!

I was really lucky that, during those first couple of years, I made dang sure that I surrounded myself with like-minded people who would lift me up when I was falling down. They helped me feel sane when things weren't going well by reminding me that it was okay to get frustrated, and that it was safe to cry and rant. They reminded me that I had a gift and my purpose was to share it with the world.

Because I had support and people who "got it," I was able to keep plugging away, and eventually learn what I needed to know to get clients and create success.

Once I took that personal inventory I told you about in Chapter 2, I realized that my concierge business was unique —and therefore needed a unique marketing strategy. I needed a plan that included in-person and virtual relationships, and that allowed the real, authentic, excitable me to shine through even when I wasn't talking with a contact face-to-face. If I could pare this plan down to the essentials, I realized, I would have a totally systematic, repeatable approach to marketing that would pretty much guarantee my success in the marketplace.

And guess what? In this chapter, I'm going to share this plan with you.

Yup. You read that right. My super-tailored system that catapulted me into my successful Concierge Life is about to unfold on these pages, just for you. Th s is your marketing superhighway, your fast-track solution to awesome visibility and amazing clients.

I don't want you to end up where I was. I don't want you to feel alone, broken, and not good enough, just because those "tried and true" old-school marketing strategies don't work for your modern concierge business!

So, are you ready? Drumroll, please ...

MY SECRET SAUCE: *The* MARKETING WHEEL

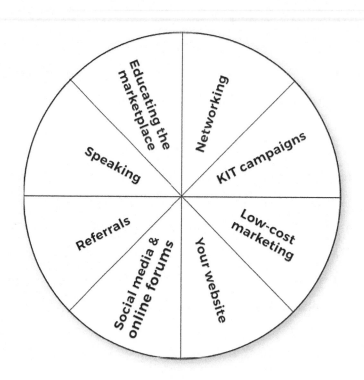

THE CONCIERGE ACADEMY
MARKETING WHEEL

When I evaluated what marketing strategies were working in my business, I found that I could break them up into eight key areas. I noticed that if I was putting my attention into all of these areas equally, using consistent and repeatable systems, my ideal clients just kept showing up.

When you sit down to formulate your marketing plan, you'll want to consider all of these areas, and think about how you can utilize them in a way that connects you with your ideal clients over, and over, and over again.

THE 8 SPOKES OF THE MARKETING WHEEL

1. Networking

Networking is the cornerstone of any successful business. You'll read so much more about this within the pages of this book, but I'm telling you now, *please* don't ignore this spoke of the wheel. Networking is about building relationships with people. Whether they become clients down the line, or trusted business advisors and power partners, you want to be present and active in your community.

It's not about going out and shoving your business cards in someone's hands. (Never do that—it's ineffective, offensive, and a waste of good business cards.) It's about starting conversations. The more people you meet and connect with, the more opportunities will open for you along the way.

As any successful person will tell you: no one becomes successful in a vacuum. Successful people end up that way based on not just their own grit, but on the people they maintain relationships with!

2. KIT (Keep in Touch) campaigns

One of the simplest marketing tools for entrepreneurs to employ—and yet, one of the most difficult and under-utilized—is to follow up and keep in touch.

Statistics are always changing. Some say it takes seven touches before someone notices you; some say that in our loud, distracted world it may take up to *nineteen* times in front of someone before they buy a product or service. Regardless of what the stats are, it's imperative to stay the course. Th s doesn't mean you have to "pester" anyone, but it does mean that you continue to nurture your relationships until they are ready to make a decision about using your services.

As I said, this is the easiest thing to do, yet the most difficult. Why? Because people fear rejection. Countless sales are lost every day because people give up after a single phone call, or two, or three. Don't take it personally if someone doesn't answer your phone call or e-mail right away, or at all. Just keep being there.

3. Low-cost marketing

Everyone wants to know how to run a concierge business "on the cheap," but if you think all you need is sweat equity to be successful, you're falling prey to one of those icky false beliefs we talked about in Chapter 2. You need cashola, pronto—but you don't have to spend six figures either. There are ways to get the word out that won't break the bank.

You can create business cards, flyers, and informational documents at a relatively low cost. If you use them consistently, you'll see much better results than if you blow all your money on a single ad in the local paper. Dollar for dollar, these simple materials provide a great return on investment. Give them out whenever you're invited to do so, and always keep a stash on hand—in your car, in your bag, and at your office (if you have one).

4. Your website

Must you have a website? (Hint: You won't like the answer!)

You don't *really* need a website if you are kicking ass with Marketing Spokes 1 through 3. Never let your lack of a web presence deter you from getting out there and building those all-important relationships.

However, as you grow, you should invest in a great website. People are finding more and more of their resources and services online these days, so even if someone's neighbor tells them about you, they're probably going to go online and look you up. When they do, you want to have a site that looks professional, functions well, and invites people to connect with you in multiple ways. You also want to have a site that makes good use of SEO, keywords, and other behind-the-scenes stuff that helps you rise to the top of the search engine results.

My advice: unless you are already a great designer/SEO expert/coder, hire someone to help you build a robust, client-attracting magnet of a website.

5. Social media and online forums

Everyone today is "on social." Use this platform as a way to educate your potential clients about what you do, who you are, and whom you serve. Use it to build credibility by sharing relevant information and inviting prospects and centers of influence to learn more about you. Reach out to people you want to connect with, and bring them into your conversations.

As fabulous as online networking is, however, it's no substitute for in-person relationship building. Nothing beats that face-to-face connection as a way to share your brand and your business with your community.

6. Referrals

This spoke of the wheel is one of my favorites! In the beginning, everything that happens in your business starts with you. All work, all clients, and all connections come from you taking action—from you giving your time, energy, and expertise.

But, as you continue to network (there's that word again) you will align with others who may not be your ideal clients, but will LOVE to send you referrals. This requires a different kind of relationship-building, and it won't happen until you put in the work to educate your referral partners and ask for their help. So if you really click with someone and trust that they're aligned and aware enough to send you clients who are truly ideal, start laying the groundwork for them to refer people to you!

7. Speaking

The easiest way to share what you do is to tell people about it. Speaking is amazing for marketing because it allows you to educate more than one person at a time. Imagine having the opportunity to share what you do with ten, fi y, even a hundred or more people! What would that do for your network?

This spoke of the wheel is certainly the most difficult for many, and I consider it a more advanced marketing strategy —but once you become comfortable talking about your business and how you make a difference for people, this strategy can be a game changer.

I promise, when you're ready to take this step, you'll get over the stage fright!

8. Educating the marketplace

Although this spoke is number 8, it's the catalyst to the entire marketing wheel. When you educate your marketplace, all of the other spokes will suddenly kick into high gear.

Marketing isn't about always being in someone's face, or paying for costly advertising; at its core, it is a tool to teach people. For as long as you live the Concierge Life, your job will be to educate potential clients and referral partners about who you are, what you do, and why it matters.

In many areas, the word "concierge" is still associated only with ritzy hotels. Just remember, once people see your passion and dedication, they will be willing to listen, learn, and connect.

Yup, that's why education is the ninja secret sauce for the whole marketing wheel!

* * * * *

Well, there it is: the secret to my success, the foundation of every marketing plan I create, and the basis for every marketing plan I develop with my Concierge Academy students. It's now yours to use in your business, every day, for as long as you live the Concierge Life.

The Marketing Wheel is simple but powerful—and it *works*. I'm living proof. If you are marketing consistently in all eight of these areas over a reasonable period of time, I guarantee that you will start spiraling toward success.

But here's the thing: if you ignore one or more of these areas, it can affect your whole outcome—especially if the areas you're neglecting are the ones that build solid relationships (like in-person networking). Remember, you can't hide behind your computer and expect to run a successful concierge business! When in doubt, always go back to the Marketing Wheel.

CONSISTENCY: THE MAGIC KEY *to* MARKETING

You've heard the phrase "consistency is key," right? But the key to what?

Here's a little gem for you: consistency is the magic key to *everything*, especially when it comes to your marketing! It unlocks every door, and breaks down every wall between you and your amazing, ideal clients.

But sadly, what I've found is that most concierge businesses tackle their marketing using the "throwing spaghetti at the wall" approach, and they never stick with anything long enough to see what, well … sticks.

It's heartbreaking, because if these businesses would just get serious about their marketing instead of flailing around with pasta in their hair, they'd be a heck of a lot more successful. Passion is great, but if you flake out before your clients get to see that passion, it doesn't do you any good.

The magic key of consistency may unlock every door, but you can grease the hinges if you also pay attention to these three things in your marketing: quality, quantity, and message.

Quality: Showcase your brand

You're not a high school student looking for odd jobs. You are selling a high-level service, and your marketing needs to reflect that. So ask yourself, "Does my marketing represent me as a high-end brand?"

More, every single representation of your business—your headshots, business cards, website, Facebook page, etc.— should scream, "I'm honest. I have integrity. I'm skilled at what I do, and I'm qualified to take on whatever you throw at me."

So if your homemade website isn't cutting it, or your

headshot is ten years old (or was taken with your bestie's iPhone and still has her shoulder in the frame), or your business cards are dripping with illegible, curly fonts and/or were printed on your home computer, you should probably take another look at your branding. Anything that doesn't immediately say "professional" has got to go.

Consistency in this area also applies to things like colors, fonts, and tone/word choices. All of your marketing materials should look (and read) like part of the same cohesive whole.

Quantity: Say it again (and again, and again)

Consistent marketing is not optional, especially in this business! In order for people to truly, completely, and instinctively understand what you do and how your services can make their lives better, you need to ABM (always be marketing).

Some studies say that people need to see something *twelve times* on digital media before they actually remember it. If you aren't consistent in this area, you won't seem present to your potential clients. In fact, you might not be more than a passing blip on the radar.

Consistency truly means being proactive about putting yourself out there—not in an "I'm gonna throw this in your face" kind of way, but in an educational, loving, caring, "I know what your struggles are" kind of way.

Message: Highlight your core concepts

Your message should be the same across all eight spokes of the Marketing Wheel. You can be creative in how you share it, and come at it from different angles, but you need to make the same point and highlight the same core concepts *each and every time* you connect with your ideal clients.

This might seem like overkill or "dumbing it down," but remember, your clients don't know your business like you do. They might not even understand what the heck you do until the tenth time they read your materials! You need to keep your messaging simple and clear so that you don't confuse people.

Truth: A confused mind never buys.

So, think about what you really want your ideal clients to know about you, your services, and your mission, and distill everything down to its core concept before you put it in your marketing.

MORE WAYS *to* IMPROVE YOUR MARKETING

There are two things that every piece of your marketing should do: break down the walls of uncertainty for your ideal clients, and make it easy for your customers to work with you.

BREAK DOWN THE WALLS OF UNCERTAINTY FOR YOUR IDEAL CLIENTS

Most people who come to a website or social media post for the first time are skeptical.

It's natural for them to feel that way. I mean, how do *you* feel when you do a Google search for a local company—especially when you're looking to hire someone to perform a service for you? I'll bet you wonder if they're as good as their website says they are. You probably wonder if they're trustworthy, if they'll show up on time, and if their services are worth the price they're charging. If the information you find about the company doesn't answer those questions, chances are you won't hire them. So why should your business be any different?

In every piece of marketing you put out there—be it a flyer, a website, a business card, or a social media post—*you must consistently convey trust and reliability*. Once you do that, you can make it easy for people to say yes.

How to build trust *before* you meet someone

As I've said before, in-person networking is the best way to get contacts and potential clients to know, like, and trust you. But what about the people who fi d you online, through your website or social media?

Here are some ways to increase your trust and reliability without ever meeting someone face-to-face:

- Put a picture of yourself on your website. (Seriously, people want to know who they're working with!)

- Put kick-ass testimonials on your website. (It's said that twenty-five testimonials is a "tipping point.") Be sure that these are real testimonials from real people. No one likes a faker.

- Use quality images on your website. If you don't have any of your own, invest in quality stock photos. Don't poach photos from Google, and don't copy and paste from other concierges' websites.

- Provide clear, relevant, free information that lets your audience get to know you.

- Make sure that all of the above are in line with your branding and message!

MAKE IT EASY FOR YOUR CUSTOMERS TO WORK WITH YOU

Have you ever gone to someone's website looking for a phone number and/or e-mail address, but can't find one? Or, the phone number rings to a voicemail box that's full, or hasn't been set up yet? *Oy vey!*

I remember going through the business cards I'd collected at a networking event, and finding the card of someone whose services interested me. My preferred method in this situation is to shoot someone an e-mail and let them get back to me at their convenience. However, when I turned over the card, there was no e-mail address.

Yes, I know that some people do this on purpose—but that doesn't change the facts. I wanted to do business with this person, but I couldn't connect with her in the way I wanted to connect (as a consumer) because she hadn't made it easy for me. Suffice to say, she didn't get my business.

The lesson here: always give your potential clients options about how to connect with you. Then, make sure those options are functional, professional, and easy to navigate.

The best part of this story, though, is that after I got over my irritation at this woman's lack of an e-mail address, I looked at my own business card and realized that my card had no e-mail address, either! (Yup. True story!) You can bet I ordered a new batch of cards that same day!

YOUR MARKETING SCHEDULE

Just this week, I pulled out my big ol' wall calendar and plotted out my marketing for the next several months.

Yes, the next *several months*. Marketing is so important to my business's success that I plan all my strategies a year in advance. That way, I can never drop the ball, or let my marketing tasks slide.

To really make it in this field, you *must* make it a priority to ABM and ABN: Always Be Marketing and Always Be Networking!

If you're not marketing and networking consistently and according to a solid strategy, you won't get the results you want. Period. So, if you don't already have your marketing tasks on your calendar, hop to it!

As you make your plan to address all 8 spokes of the Marketing Wheel, think about:

- When and where you will network in person. (Remember, get out there at least eight times per month!)

- When you will upload new blog articles.

- When you will post on social media. (Hint: automatic scheduling tools are awesome!)

- When and where you will distribute your low-cost marketing (LCM) materials.

Then, get it all on your calendar, for as many weeks or months in advance as you can.

THE 6 WORDS *that* WILL KILL YOUR BUSINESS

A good friend of mine, who is also an entrepreneur, hit a bump in her concierge business. She wasn't getting as many clients as she would have liked. So, of course, I dove right in and started coaching her.

The first thing I asked was, "Are you following up?"

"Well, I sent an e-mail, but no one responded."

"Okay, I know that sucks. But it happens all the time. What did you do next? Did you try to reach out again? Did you put a process in place to follow up with them every month?"

Her response? "They know where to fi d me." *Whaaaaat?*

Remember, consistency is the magic key to success in your business. You always need to follow up—and you need to keep following up until that potential client hires you or asks you to "please, go away!"

Have you ever heard that quote about stopping three feet from gold? Th s is what I'm talking about.

Just this past week, we worked with a client who needed to get her office in order. She had been putting it off for months, and it was impacting her personal productivity. So, we organized and rearranged her office to make the space work for her. She was thrilled. Like, gushing. She couldn't believe she had waited so long to hire us.

When I looked at my records, I saw that I had been checking in with her for two years. *Two friggin' years.* And not once did I think, "She knows where to find me."

Those six words—"They know where to find me"—are the six words that will kill your business.

As a service professional it is your job to help your clients find you. That way, they can get the help they need when they are finally ready to say yes.

So, today (or before the end of this week), I want you to go back through your e-mails and all the notes you've taken about potential leads who've said, "Not now," and follow up. Tell them you're sorry for not being in touch sooner, but that you're here for them now, and you'd love to continue the conversation at their convenience.

If you're resisting this, ask yourself, "What matters more to me: my fear of rejection or my desire to succeed as a concierge?"

Yup. It's all or nothing, my friend. You do the work—even when it's uncomfortable—or you don't get clients.

ABOVE ALL, DON'T WAIT UNTIL YOU "GET IT RIGHT!"

Don't allow perfection to stop you from getting out there. As I've said before, it can take several months or even years until people are ready to say "yes" to getting help in their lives. And, because people want to hire people they know, like, and trust, they need that "courtship" period before they are ready to take the leap into a working relationship. That can't happen if you're hiding behind your computer and trying to perfect your business cards.

The point is, now is the best time to get out there. Yes, you want your business cards to look nice, but the best place for potential clients to hear your message is straight out of your mouth. When I tracked where our clients have found us over the past year, I discovered that 75 percent came to us through connections I made while networking.

The great thing is, the more you talk to other people face-to-face about your business, the clearer you'll get about your message and how your potential clients receive it. Then, you can take what you learn and apply it to all of the other areas of your marketing.

Your business will evolve with time. My branding has gone through four (yes, count 'em: *four*) evolutions in the last several years. If I had waited until I "got it right" before I put myself out there, I wouldn't be in business today.

The BIG LESSON

As a concierge, marketing is your #1 job. So do what you need to do to love your work!

Dive in to this learning process and find out the best ways to reach your ideal clients so you can help more people.

- Study the Marketing Wheel and beef up your strategies in those areas you've been neglecting.

- Streamline your branding and marketing materials.

- Schedule your marketing tasks as far in advance as possible so you don't drop the ball.

If marketing feels scary or out of reach for you, reach out for help. Not sure where to get started with your marketing? Let us help with The Concierge Starter Kit. You can get your own Concierge Starter Kit by going to www.theconciergeacademy.com/starterkit.

Now, let's move on to our next challenge: your business mindset!

Chapter 4

THE CONCIERGE MINDSET

"WHO DOES SHE THINK SHE IS, ANYWAY?"

Those were the words I was most afraid to hear when I started my concierge business—and, to be honest, I still cringe a little inside if I think people are judging me. I wonder: are they comparing themselves to me, or trying to compete with me? Sometimes I even feel like people are looking at me and asking themselves that dreaded question, "Who does she think she is?"

Some days though, it's the voices of the "inner critics" that are actually far worse. When I have my down-on-myself moments, those voices love to shout things like, "You're not smart enough to do this. You'll never make it. Why don't you just get a real job?" Oh, and my favorite, "You're not special."

I know I'm not the only one who's ever felt like this.

Fear, doubt, anxiety, apathy, impatience, frustration, anger… They happen to everyone at some point. The difference between "everyone" and successful business owners is *how those feelings get managed.*

If you're not feeling on top of your game, your business won't thrive. It's your job to keep your head, and your heart, up.

The three biggest hurdles for any concierge business owner are *fear,* *overwhelm,* and *impatience.* In order to keep these three things from sabotaging your business, you need to develop your confidence, learn how to use your time wisely (so that you're successfully marketing), and—most of all—have patience.

In this chapter, I'm going to give you some tools that will help you get beyond these hurdles and reset your mindset so you can live your ultimate Concierge Life.

CONQUER *Your* FEAR: A 3-STEP MINDSET RESET

As you've learned in Chapters 1 through 3 of this book, your most important job as a concierge is to market your business. But here's another secret for you: if your mindset is in the crapper, even your most brilliant marketing strategies won't work.

Why? Because *you are your brand*. And when you're not feeling like the shining star on your company's stage, you'll hold yourself back from doing what needs to be done to get out there and tell your ideal clients exactly how you can help them. When you don't feel like that rockstar, you won't take action. You won't say yes to opportunities.

If you keep hearing the nagging voice of your inner critic, it's a sign that you need to take a step back from the hustle for a few minutes, and remember why the heck you started this business in the first place! Marketing is your most important job in your business, but ultimately, it's not why you became a concierge.

You help people. That's what you do.

And you're *great* at it.

When I get overwhelmed by the cranky voices in my head, or feel totally held back by fear, or when I'm sitting there with my arms crossed like a little kid, saying, "I don't wanna! I'm scared!" I use this simple 3-step process to get myself back on track and feeling like a rockstar again. Because, look: we aren't here just to live any old life. We're here to live the Concierge Life—and in order to do that, we *must* take control of our own minds!

My 3-step Mindset Reset

1. Review your testimonials

2. Remember your "why"

3. Feel the fear, and do it anyway!

When I do these three simple things, it helps me get back in my groove. Sometimes I can reset in less than an hour; some days, it might take me a bit longer. But I have learned how to step away from the negativity and realign myself so I can move forward. And, the more you do this work, the easier it will become. I promise!

MINDSET RESET STEP #1: REVIEW YOUR TESTIMONIALS

A while back, I created a special folder in my e-mail and named it my "happy file." Th s is where I save love notes from clients, team members who love working for me, and people who "just wanted to drop you a note to say how much I love your weekly tips and strategies."

By reviewing the kind words of others, I remember why I chose this career after working for decades in healthcare. The kindness of others and the knowledge of how I have positively impacted their lives fills my bucket.

So, save those little love notes, because they can literally pull you back from the brink when you're having a bad week.

In addition to your "happy file," create a "happy box" or "love box." In my office, I have a beautiful wooden box that holds all the handwritten thank you cards and notes I've received over the years. When you are fighting to keep your head clear, find a space that feels good (maybe outside under a tree, or in your bathroom with the door locked), open your "love box," and feel the gratitude pour off those notes and into your heart.

MINDSET RESET STEP #2: REMEMBER YOUR "WHY"

Look, being an entrepreneur, especially in a service field, is *not* easy. I'll bet your family doesn't get you, and most of your friends probably don't get you either. They may support you, but they don't know what it's like to face the music day after day in this industry. They don't know what it's like to start a business from scratch, and be solely responsible for every bit of work that comes through the door. They don't understand what's it's like to be the CEO, marketer, bookkeeper, administrative assistant, and service provider all at the same time!

Let's face it: most of us didn't end up in this business because we like wearing three hundred hats every day. We became concierges because we love helping other people, and we are great at "GSD" (Getting Shit Done).

Our mission: to be catalysts for positive change in other people's lives, and improve people's quality of life.

Serving others is our "why." It's what gets us out of bed in the morning, and gives us the courage to stand up in front of fifty (or five hundred) strangers and talk about what we do and why it matters. It's why we chose this work, and why we keep working it.

You started this business for a very specific reason. Maybe you took care of your dad as he was aging, and now you want to help others do the same. Perhaps you watched your mom work herself to the bone trying to hold down a job, raise kids, and keep a household running, and you want to prevent other kids from losing their "mom time" to errands. Perhaps your mission in life is to help bring families together again at the dinner table, or save other solopreneurs from drowning in their office clutter. Maybe it's simply to pay for a new car or contribute to your family's grocery budget.

We all have our own "why." The only qualification is that your "why" needs to be strong enough to keep you moving forward when things aren't easy-breezy. So, get to know your "why." Feel it. Write it out on a Post-it, and stick it right on your computer screen or the wall in your office. Even just a few words like "Family meals," or "Aging with grace and dignity" will be enough to remind you why you chose the Concierge Life.

Hold onto that "why," my friend. It's the gas in your tank.

MINDSET RESET STEP #3:
FEEL THE FEAR, AND DO IT ANYWAY

I love this one (even though, in the moment, I hate doing it).

I learned this from one of my mentors years ago, who told us, "Feel the fear, and do it anyway." The trouble is, the first part is automatic, but the second part isn't always easy.

Fear can consume you if you let it. What if they make fun of you? What if you're not good enough? What if, what if, what if … I've heard all the "what if's" you can think of in my own head at one time or another. I was so good at "what if" that I nearly "what iffed" myself out of business!

But after facing my fears time after time, over the course of several years, I learned something very important: *fear is actually a gift.*

Fear only jumps up and down in your face when you're about to push through a boundary. Fear's job is to keep you "safe," and anything that feels new, bigger, or different— even if your rational mind knows it will be awesome—makes fear scream louder.

So, what do you do when you feel so scared you can't "do it anyway?" Give yourself permission to feel the fear, terror, and anxiety—but put a time limit on it. (Seriously. If you have to, set an alarm!) Give yourself fifteen minutes. Let your inner critic screech. Let your fear do its dance. Cry, rant, and hide under your blankets. Reach out to your circle of entrepreneurial friends, the people who help hold you up when everything else seems to be falling apart. Then, when that timer goes off, do what you have to do to move forward.

BONUS NINJA STRATEGY: TAKE ACTION

When you find yourself in a situation where procrastination or fear has a crippling hold on you, there is only one thing you really need to do: take action!

Don't try to tackle the entire situation. Just take one tiny step forward. You know that saying that goes, "You can't be in faith and fear at the same time?" Well, you can't be in action and fear at the same time, either! Every time you take action, you take a mini leap of faith—which moves you away from fear.

KILL *the* OVERWHELM: CLEAR *the* DECKS

You're great at GSD ... for other people. But when it comes to your business, it might feel like a different story. You're scattered, rushing from task to task, and the more items you tick off your to-do list, the more seem to get added. Every day feels like a whirlwind.

One of the biggest factors in burnout in this business (or

any business) is overwhelm. When you feel like there's too much to do, you have trouble setting priorities. First, little things start to fall through the cracks; then, big things follow. Soon, you feel like you're drowning in stuff that needs to be done—and *all* of it feels like a priority!

As I mentioned in Chapter 2, delegation is magic. But if you're not organizing your own time, delegating to someone else won't solve the feelings of stress and overwhelm. In fact, delegation itself might feel like a burden on your time!

If this sounds familiar, it might be time for you to "clear the decks!"

I learned this from my mentor and business coach several years ago. When I did this, it skyrocketed my productivity.

Without structure in your day, you'll find yourself overwhelmed with that feeling of "What do I need to do next?" If you don't organize your time, you might end up filling big chunks of your day with unimportant (or less-important) tasks that get in the way of your big goals. The idea behind "clearing the decks" is to eliminate time-wasters and learn to say no to disruptions. That way, you can prioritize the tasks that really matter to your success (ahem, *marketing*), and stop giving your time away to things that don't help you grow your business.

One of the things I teach my students in The Concierge Academy is how to plan out their weeks with a healthy combination of marketing time, client time (when you provide your services), and family/reboot time. So, open up your calendar for the week, and schedule in all the tasks that are important to your business, and need to get done. I'm talking marketing, follow-up calls, coffee dates with potential clients, etc. Even if you plan to spend all day at your desk, block out times for specific tasks. Then, commit to doing *only those things* during the times you've blocked.

Seems simple, right? It is ... and it isn't. In order to create this type of consistent structure in your life and business, you have to set firm boundaries around your time, and be extra picky about what activities you say yes (or no) to.

This means not taking phone calls during your marketing hours, even if they are from potential clients. It means ignoring your inbox while you're working on your social media, and vice versa. It means never opening Facebook or Twitter during work hours unless you are posting for your business. It means asking your kids not to disturb you while you're mapping out your marketing strategy, and bookmarking that interesting news article to read in your free time. It means saying no to PTA meetings (at least, while you're ramping up your business), cutting out TV time, and ix-naying other activities that don't help you grow your business.

In the early days, I used to take two hours out of the middle of my day to shower and exercise. Then, I figured out that those were prime networking and marketing hours, and I was missing out! Yes, exercise and showers are truly necessary—but they can easily happen before my work day begins. Now, I start my day with a workout and spend the lunch hours working my marketing magic.

Other things that got cut from my workday schedule: random grocery store runs, online shopping, and post office visits. All of those could be done outside of my scheduled work hours—or outsourced.

With practice, "clearing the decks" will get easier, and you'll learn to prioritize more effectively. You'll also feel a heck of a lot less overwhelmed, which in turn will help keep you from sliding into fear and burnout.

So, start "clearing the decks," and watch a mountain of possibilities unfold for you.

COPING *with* "N O"

One of the biggest disappointments when selling your services is hearing that two-letter word, *no*.

But here's the thing: many times, "no" doesn't really mean no. It just means, "not now."

The people you're talking to might not be ready to hire you right now. Maybe they don't know, like, and trust you enough yet. Maybe they're afraid to delegate. Maybe they can't wrap their heads around what you do and how you can help them. (Hint: Your marketing message should address those last two!)

Our business is based on deep, personal relationships. That's where it all begins. Our clients become friends, even family. But it doesn't happen overnight.

I remember feeling heartbroken that I was having so many conversations, but getting so few new clients. My sales pitches were not converting. I kept beating myself up for my "failures."

When we talk to ourselves this way, we lose our confidence. When we lose confidence, we can't market our business with integrity and enthusiasm—and that sends us into a downward spiral of less business and more negativity. No thank you!

It took me a while, but I finally realized that the day I met someone didn't have to be the day they said yes to me. That one truth totally relieved my anxiety. It wasn't that I was doing something wrong, or that people didn't like me, or that I wasn't good enough. It was just that my ideal clients needed more time to get to know, like, and trust me—and, even more so, learn how to use our services!

So, be patient. Remind yourself that a client who says yes can become a client for life—and a client for life is worth waiting a couple of extra weeks or months (or even years) for.

In the meantime, start tracking what you are doing to move your business forward, and look back every once in a while to see how far you've come. You'll begin to see some very cool patterns—and, chances are, you've grown more than you thought you had.

BONUS NINJA STRATEGY: INVEST IN YOUR MINDSET

Whether they're on the medal stand at the Olympics or claiming their Superbowl rings, great athletes always credit their coaches for instilling the discipline necessary to achieve a goal and providing encouragement during those oh-so-difficult times.

The same is true for entrepreneurs! We need someone on our team who can see the big picture—someone who isn't down in the trenches of the day-to-day. More, we need someone who has already done what we want to do, and created the growth and success we want for ourselves.

I used to go to networking events and hear people talk about their coaches. I didn't get it. I was very new to entrepreneurship, and still thought I could do it all and then some. After I hired those first couple of coaches, I *still* didn't get it. I mean, they helped me some, but they weren't giving me the same kind of "wow" support that my colleagues always raved about when they talked about their own coaches.

The truth is, a coach can be your greatest asset in business. But if you don't take the time to find the right coach, you won't reap the benefits.

The year I hired my "wow" coach was the same year I took on a full-time team member. It was a huge leap of faith. I was now going to pay someone else to take care of my clients, plus dish out five figures a year for this high-level coach … I felt like my head was going to explode. But deep inside, I knew I had to do it. I had to invest in myself, and do whatever it took to see myself as the rockstar entrepreneur everyone else claimed to see when they looked at me. I had to get out of my own way.

That time, I chose the right coach, and I got the "wow" support I'd been longing for. I just had to go beyond my comfort zone to find her!

When you're looking for a coach, you need to ask a couple of very important questions, and answer them honestly. Otherwise, you'll end up where I did those first couple of times, paying big money for support that wasn't really what I needed.

So, to save you the frustration I went through those first couple of years, here are my 5 Key Questions to Ask Before You Hire a Business Coach.

5 KEY QUESTIONS TO ASK BEFORE YOU HIRE A BUSINESS COACH

1. What do I really need help with?
2. Is this coach compatible with me?
3. Is this coach five steps ahead of me?
4. Does this coach have amazing references?
5. Can this coach give me honest, objective feedback?

Question #1: What do I really need help with?

A business coach can assist with things as specific as identifying ideal clients, pricing your services, how to have an effective sales conversation, or how to make the most of networking opportunities. Determine those areas in which you need the most help, and make a commitment to fi ding a qualified expert.

Question #2: Is this coach compatible with me?

Personalities don't always click. You can meet three different people who teach the exact same stuff, but only one gets through to you on a core level. What makes coaching effective is the partnership you create with your coach. So, the perfect business coach for you might not always be the one everyone else is flocking to.

For example: I am loving and giving in my coaching, but I will also call you out when I hear you making excuses, or see you getting in your own way. Not everyone likes that, and that's okay! Your business coach should be someone who earns your trust and confidence, and never intimidates you into following their advice.

Question #3: Is this coach five steps ahead of me?

The most valuable experience is *real* experience. So, find someone who has already gone where you want to go, but isn't so far down the road that they can't look back and understand where you are.

Question #4: Does this coach have amazing references?

Before you hire a business coach, be sure to check their references. Review this coach's testimonials. Do a Google search. Reach out to, and follow up with, people who have worked with the coach before (not just people who know of him/her or go to the same networking groups). Current and former clients can tell you what worked and what didn't, and share ideas about how to get the most out of your coaching experience.

Question #5: Can this coach give me honest, objective feedback?

As an entrepreneur, you can count on friends and family members for many things—but don't expect honest criticism to be among them.

Your business coach should be someone who is fair, reasonable, and interested in your success, but also willing to tell the truth, even if it's not what you want to hear. Remember, we don't grow from the status quo!

The BIG LESSON

Your mindset, and how you manage your big emotions, has a lot to do with your success as a concierge. In this chapter, I've given you some tips for keeping your fear, overwhelm, and impatience in check, so you can keep growing your business, serving your clients, and creating your Concierge Life.

Next up? How to create (and price) services in that "sweet spot" that will have your niche clients' ears perking up and your phone ringing.

Ready ... set ... go!

Chapter 5

NICHE SERVICES (AND WHY THEY MATTER)

YOU CAN'T BE ALL THINGS TO ALL PEOPLE.

I know, I know: you've heard it all before. You've probably read a variation of that statement in every one of those marketing books now collecting dust on your shelves. But although I don't put much faith in the usual marketing wisdom (as you may have guessed), this tidbit is 100 percent true and accurate.

You really can't please everyone. If you try, you'll people-please yourself right into burnout and even out of business.

Trust me, I know.

You fell in love with the Concierge Life because you wanted to make a specific impact for specific people. If you want to *stay* in love with your Concierge Life and build a business that feels fulfilling, you need to do two things:

1. Identify your ideal clients, and

2. Create services targeted to those clients.

It's a fact that when you don't know who your ideal client is, you will waste lots of emotional energy, time, and fiancial resources shouting to the masses. And quite frankly, the masses have *no idea* how to work with you.

That's why a solid Ideal Client Profile is the foundation of all successful concierge businesses, and the source of all great marketing. It's also why, in my Concierge Academy, one of the first assignments I give my students is creating their ideal client profile in painstaking detail.

So sit back, close your eyes, and picture the person you would give anything to work with. Who do you see?

WHO IS *Your* IDEAL CLIENT?

I've mentioned the idea of "ideal clients" before in this book; now, it's time to find out who those people actually are, so you can start crafting services and packages that will really light them up.

Your ideal clients are people who:

- You love working with.
- Need the services you enjoy providing.
- Are willing and able to pay for your services.

Simple, right? Well, kinda.

In the beginning, it's quite hard to know who your ideal clients are because you don't have much experience yet. I mean, how can you pinpoint your ideal client when you haven't actually worked with an ideal client yet? If you're not aware of this, it can create a whole lot of confusion for you.

I see so many people come into this business with a dream to help one specific group of people, but lose their way when they don't get clients quickly enough or don't market to the right people. All of a sudden, they start saying things like, "I don't really like doing X, but I have to do it to pay the bills until I get the clients I really want to work with."

When I started, I was just like you. I took on any legal and ethical gig thrown my way! I created a resume for someone. I worked on a PowerPoint presentation and database files. (Okay, I actually paid my neighbor to do that stuff because I had no clue what I was doing and she was brilliant at it! But she also had a job and a family, so bugging her for help was only a short-term solution!) Point is, I had no idea who I really wanted to serve, or how to reach them, so I tried to be a jack of all trades.

Th s is backwards thinking. I mean, what do you think the word-of-mouth about your services is going to be if you do jobs you don't like for people who aren't your ideal clients to begin with? What types of clients do you think those not-so-ideal clients are going to refer? If you start taking jobs you dislike just to make a buck, it's like false advertising. When you fi ally start saying, "I don't really do that," people are going to feel cheated. Plus, you're going to start to hate your job—and that would be tragic.

I'm not saying you can't make exceptions for certain clients or awesome opportunities. But for the most part, trying to be everything to everyone only leaves you frustrated.

So before you start putting yourself out there, get as clear an idea as possible about who your ideal clients are and what you want to do for them.

When creating your Ideal Client Profile[1], here are some key points to consider:

- Male or female (or doesn't matter)?
- Local or tourist/snowbird?
- Lifestyle and activities?
- Rural, suburban, or urban?
- Age group?

(1) Ninja Bonus: Check out the Ideal Client Worksheet on page 136!

- Married or single?

- Kids or no kids?

- Occupation? (Business owner, corporate employee, stay-at-home mom, retiree, etc.)

- Likes & dislikes?

- Personality and personal qualities?

- Biggest problems or concerns right now (that you can help with)?

I could write a list of questions five pages long, but you get the idea. You truly can't be too specific

You can also make a separate list of qualities you don't want in your ideal clients. For example, you might not want to work with people who are pushy, argumentative, or set in their ways. Or, you might not want to work with people who are indecisive, or need excessive hand-holding.

Once you have created a profile, ask yourself if the avatar you've sketched out actually meets the three primary qualifications for your ideal client. Will you love working with him/her? Does this person need the services you want to provide? And, most importantly, is this person willing and able to pay you?

That last one is another place where new concierges (and sometimes experienced ones) get tripped up. It's not just about who you want to work with; it's about whether the people you want to work with can afford to work with you.

The reality is, if you want your business to stay open, you must charge—and willingly accept—payment for your services. I used to say to my husband, "If no one is willing to pay me, I should just become a nonprofit and give my services away for free!" (I forgot, in that moment, that nonprofits rely on donations, and that instead of asking people to give me money in exchange for a service, I'd be asking them to give me money for nothing but a tax deduction! Gulp!)

Here's the hard truth: *if your ideal clients aren't able to pay you, they are not your ideal clients.*

I worked with a startup concierge about a year ago who was super-passionate about helping single moms. It was all she talked about. Why? Because she had been that single mom, and now she felt like it was her time to give back. But here's the thing: she wasn't getting any clients, because the single moms she was focused on could barely make ends meet, let alone afford a concierge!

As we worked together, I coached to pivot just a little and focus on serving "corporate" single moms who had recently gone through divorce. These women not only needed her services desperately, they could easily afford them. Now, she has the consistent clients and income she needs to run a profitable business, and can donate her services once a month to a mom who normally would not be able to afford them.

That's the impact knowing your ideal client inside and out can have on your business.

So, if you feel really passionate about serving a particular group and keep coming up with ideal client profiles that don't fit the bill (literally), you might want to go back to the drawing board and pivot your profile to align with people who can actually pay you. Then, come up with a plan to donate your services (or fundraise to cover your expenses) to the group you originally intended to serve.

NICHE MARKETING:
A PROFITABLE PIPELINE

You probably felt a little cringe inside when you did the exercise on the previous pages. It's scary to narrow things down so far, especially when you're just starting out. You may be dealing with the fear that there aren't enough clients to go around, especially when you niche down with laser precision.

What you don't realize is that trying to marketing to a broad demographic dilutes your message and your access. Your marketing becomes much more time-consuming and cash-wasting, and you'll end up spreading yourself too thin. You can't saturate all possible markets on a startup budget unless you have a trust fund (and even then, it's a bad idea.) This was one of the biggest marketing mistakes I made when starting out, and it cost me big—not only in dollars, but in mental exhaustion.

When you know who your ideal clients are—and when your Ideal Client Profile fits the three criteria above—you will also know three very important things:

- Who to market to.
- How to market to them.
- How to price your services.

So, take that picture you've created of your ideal client, and use it to pick and choose the best possible marketing strategies in all areas of your Marketing Wheel. (Hint: you can actually fi d a photo that represents this ideal client and keep it front of you when you're marketing!) Use the tips I shared in Chapter 3 to create a marketing message and strategy that speaks to exactly what your ideal clients need, want, and will pay for.

Ask yourself, "What are my ideal client's biggest pain points? And how can I solve them by providing services I love to do and get excited about?" Then, craft your marketing message and USP (Unique Selling Proposition) to educate your ideal clients about what their problems are and how you can solve them.

I'll give you an example of how this works.

At Task Complete, we specialize in senior companion visits. We work exclusively with seniors who do not require personal care but need a helping hand to continue to live life to the fullest on their own terms. We are the ones people call when home care is not the alternative solution. Our ideal clients want to build a relationship with one companion and retain the ability to control how they use that companion's services.

We engage our clients in everyday activities that fuel their sense of worth and involvement. This helps them feel younger and thrive more, because through personalized engagement they can live a life that is still active and meaningful. Our clients experience more joy, and their families receive peace of mind.

As you can see, the "pain point" for our ideal clients is the desire to live a fulfilling, meaningful, active life, but not having the ability to do it on their own. We solve that problem by providing personalized services that seniors can adapt to meet the needs of the active lifestyle they want to create.

Boom. Sold.

Your ideal clients might be stay-at-home moms, busy families, corporate bigwigs, solopreneurs, seniors, disabled people, or any other group of people on the planet. If you can speak directly to their wants, needs, dreams, and goals in your marketing, you will attract your ideal clients.

The BIG LESSON

You're doing a lot of work right now to identify your ideal client and niche market. But here's the thing: your ideal client will change over time!

The more clients you work with, the more you'll start to recognize and identify people who really make your days amazing. As your business grows, you'll meet more and more of these clients, and you'll be able to craft niche services that serve them in ways they didn't even realize they needed.

That doesn't mean that if you get a call to pick up a lamp and ship it across the country to Washington State (true story!) you can't do it. All it means is that more and more of your time will be spent doing things you really love, for people you really care about. That's the Concierge Life at its best.

Now, it's time to take the knowledge you've gained about your ideal client and use it to put a price tag on not only the services you will offer, but the value you're bringing to the table.

Chapter 6

OWN YOUR VALUE

"SO, WHAT DO YOU CHARGE?"

Oh, man. That can be a hard question to answer, no matter what industry you're in or what you're selling. When I started out, I got asked that question a lot, and I always ended up mumbling or stammering my answer, because I was afraid the response would be, "What? You can't charge that much! Who do you think you are?"

There it is again: "*Who do you think you are?*" You are a professional service provider who provides value beyond what dollars can measure. Your services give people back their time and their sanity. You help people free up space to follow their own goals and actually enjoy their lives.

What do *you* think that's worth?

To me, it's priceless. But since we're in business, we need to put a cash value on what we do. And that can be really, *really* hard—especially when you're first starting out. Before you can put a price tag on your services, you need to connect with and own your value as a concierge.

HOW TO ALIGN YOUR VALUE *with* YOUR SERVICES

Your ideal clients—the ones who actually want to hire you and build a relationship with you—are looking for more than just a price. They are looking for the value you provide. So instead of looking simply at an arbitrary hourly rate or income goal, start to consider what the services you offer are worth in terms of your clients' benefit.

When people hire you, they aren't just blindly hiring someone to "do stuff." Th ey are looking for someone to create a specific outcome in one or more areas of their lives. So, while the service you perform might seem small (like running errands or cleaning out a garage) the *value* of your service is more family time, more income-generating work time, or greater peace of mind.

Here's a list of questions to consider when creating your pricing structure. Remember, it's all about the value you bring to the table, and the outcome and benefit to your clients.

- What expertise do you have (whether from your personal life or a previous career)?

- What sets you apart from the crowd? What is your unique skill set?

- What is your productivity level? Are you highly efficient?

- What personal connections do you have that can add value to your clients' lives?

- What is your influence level within your industry and community?

- How do you complete tasks and correspond with your clients? How is this different than the way others might do things?

- Do you have a team? What extra value does each of your team members bring to the table?

When you sit down to price out your services, please don't think, "I'll just do what everyone else does." You are a unique person, with unique skills and a unique business model. Your business serves a different population of clients than other concierge businesses. (And now you know who that population is, thanks to our work in Chapter 5!) If you're catering to wealthy suburbanites, you're going to price your services differently than someone who wants to work with the elderly in rural areas.

You'll also need to consider where you're operating. If you're based in a small suburban town in the Midwest, you probably won't be able to charge the same rates as a concierge in New York City or southern California. That said, while demographics do play a role, they are not the be-all, end-all of the pricing conundrum. In the end, it's all about the value you bring and what your ideal clients are willing and able to pay.

So, let's get a bit clearer on that all-important question of what to charge.

THREE WAYS TO PRICE YOUR SERVICES

In The Concierge Academy, we dive deep into the question of pricing, and create a unique pricing structure for each and every student based on ideal client demographics, goals, business models, and individual services. Of course, it's pretty much impossible for me to do that in this format, since we can't have a conversation on this page—but I would love to share with you three basic ways to price your services that have been part of my own business model over the years.

These are just three of the many possibilities you could choose to explore when creating your services and packages, but they're a great place to start, and I know they work in the real world.

Service Model #1: Á la carte

As your business grows, you may notice that people will ask you to do specific tasks on an as-needed basis. In these situations, you can price the job based on what the client wants. Th s could be a flat project fee or an hourly rate. (You may even create a pre-set *à la carte* menu based on repeat requests.)

This pricing model is great for one-off jobs, but not so good at building long-term client relationships. Still, *à la carte* services have their place—and they're a great way for new clients to get to know you and see how you work.

If you choose to make *à la carte* services a part of what you offer, I recommend that you only take on tasks that you really want to do, and that you have the skill set for. If you want to build a niche as a personal shopper and curator, cleaning out someone's office is *not* a great way to show off your skills!

Service Model #2: Bulk hourly packages

This is a great way to work when clients have larger projects or aren't sure exactly how they want to use your services (yet). In these cases, you can create a "package" of hours that can be used however your client wants. Then, it's up to you to educate them about how those hours can be used!
Get creative here. What types of service packages would your ideal clients jump up and down over? Small packages

of five or ten hours? Or larger packages of twenty or forty hours? Think about the services you love to provide and how long it takes for you to complete them. Then, create packages that match that time frame.

I also highly recommend putting a time frame around when these hours can be used. For example, you might require that the hours be used within six months, or one year. Otherwise, you might have someone coming back to you six years from now to use up those last two hours! (Bet you can't guess how I know this!)

Regardless, this pricing model is great when you need a quick cash infusion. You can sell up front, and deliver later. Smart, right? You can highlight bulk hourly packages when you're gathering cash to make an investment that will take your business to the next level.

Service Model #3: Retainer packages

In this type of program, clients sign up for a set number of hours each and every month, quarter, or even year. They then sign a contract with you, and pay a set fee on an agreed-upon schedule. These contracts can range from a few hundred dollars to a few thousand dollars. (I've even created a $50,000 package!)

This model is the best for long-term growth and profitability. Why? Because you know what your income will be each month, and how many hours you will need to spend with your clients, so you can plan much more effectively! If bulk hourly packages are your cash bonus, retainer packages are your monthly salary.

When you create retainer packages, you'll want to be sure that you are offering your clients amazing value and perks for investing in your services. (Hint: this is why they will want to do business with you year after year!) Ask yourself what you can add in as a bonus or perk that you wouldn't share with your *à la carte* or bulk hours clients. For smaller retainers, it might be fresh flowers delivered to their home once a month. For big contracts, it might be bonus hours or special "pampering" services. The bonuses you offer will be commensurate with the size of the retainer package—but no matter what you decide to do, your highest priority should be to make your retainer clients feel *über* special.

DISCOUNTS? *HELL*, NO!

When you're first starting out and struggling to get clients, it's tempting to discount your services to get people to bite. Ditto for when a sales conversation isn't going as smoothly as you'd hoped. But when it comes to offering discounts, I have two words for you: *Hell*, no!

Do not discount your rates, no matter how tempting it might be.

When you discount your services, three things will inevitably happen:

1. You will inevitably attract the wrong clients—the people who don't value what you offer enough to pay full price for it.

2. The perceived value of your services will drop. Remember, you're not just selling services; you're solving problems for people. When you slash your prices, you're also saying, "The value I offer isn't worth the higher price."

3. You will resent your clients. Every hour you spend with them will feel longer, because you're not getting paid what you know you're worth.

So, I'll say it again: *Do not* discount your services. Instead, offer incentives!

Think bonuses, free gifts, and thoughtful touches—just like we talked about in the section on retainer packages. Offer these for a limited time, or to a limited number of people. You'll attract new clients who are excited about the value you're providing but won't balk at your rates.

Need more help with your pricing? We have a video training course available. Get your pricing video training by going to https://theconciergeacademy.com/pricing.

HOW MUCH IS TOO MUCH?

You've heard the old saying, "Never let 'em see you sweat?" Th s applies to your rates, too.

A couple of years into my business, my coach told me to up my rates. My first thought was, "No one will pay that!" But I felt the fear and did it anyway—and I got a bunch of new clients.

Then, that coach told me to up my rates again. But this time, the magic didn't happen. I had lots of sales conversations, but none were converting.

Why? Because I wasn't comfortable asking for that higher rate! I couldn't (yet) reconcile the value of what I was offering with this larger dollar amount. I didn't believe in myself enough to own my value at that level—and it showed!

This conundrum is called an "energetic snag." The rate change wasn't the first one I hit, or the last, but it did teach me something: your prospects can smell your fear.

Have you ever had a conversation with someone you wanted to hire, but they couldn't seem to give you a straight answer on the price? Did they drop their eyes when they gave the quote? Stutter when they told you their hourly rate? Chances are, they were in an energetic snag, just like I was.

If you can't comfortably stand by your rate, that's a sign that you need to build your confidence. (And maybe your testimonial list, too!) So choose a rate that you can stand by comfortably, without flinching, but without undervaluing yourself, either. Stay at that rate until you feel more confident that what you are offering is, in fact, worth more. Then, increase your rates, and stay at this new level until you become comfortable there again.

The BIG LESSON

Owning your value is a process. It forces you to process your fear and flex your confidence muscles. It's not easy, but it's something you need to do. After all, you want to create an awesome Concierge Life, not a so-so concierge business!

In the next chapter, we'll take a look at how you can take your perfectly-priced services list and use it to fast-track your profits and take the fastest path to cash!

Chapter 7

THE FASTEST PATH TO CASH

AS YOU'VE PROBABLY GUESSED, the fastest path to cash in your concierge business is to become an expert marketer! Put your energy into marketing, first and foremost, and you'll be on the fast track to getting clients and creating that all-important referral network.

"But," you might be asking, "What's the best way to market when I need a cash infusion?"

The best way to market is the one that gets you in front of as many of your ideal clients as possible. So while all the spokes of the Marketing Wheel are important to your marketing strategy, in the beginning, you will want to put most of your time, energy, and resources into these four areas.

YOUR TOP 4 MARKETING STRATEGIES

1. Networking

2. Speaking for visibility

3. COIs (Centers of Influence)

4. KIT (Keep-In-Touch) campaigns

#1: Networking

Remember when I told you in Chapter 1 that you need to be networking eight times a month, minimum? I meant it. Being present and visible amongst your potential clients is the *best* way to get business, hands down. The more time you spend with people face-to-face, the more you'll be able to build up your KLT (Know, Like, and Trust) factor, your credibility, and your name recognition.

I've said it before, and I'll say it again: effective networking is the number one way to grow your concierge business.

#2: Speaking

Get out and speak to groups and educate your marketplace about what you do and who you serve. If possible, speak to groups that contain as many of your ideal clients or potential COIs as possible.

Which brings us to …

#3: COIs (Centers of Influence)

A Center of Influence is someone in your network who can easily refer business to you. A COI is most often someone who works with the same clients you do, but have a non-competing business. Networking and speaking are great ways to connect with potential COIs and build relationships.

#4: KIT (Keep-In-Touch) campaigns

As you'll remember from Chapter 3, a Keep-In-Touch campaign is a system you put in place to consistently attract and follow up with clients and referral partners/COIs. Follow up with everyone, as many times as it takes. Remember that "they know where to find me" are six words that will kill your business!

If you want to build relationships and start growing your business fast, focus on these four key areas! Make sure you're scheduling these activities on your calendar consistently—as in, *every day*—and following through on all the positive connections you make. Track your successes and celebrate every new connection you make, even if that connection doesn't turn into a paying client right off the bat.

HOW TO BE *a* NINJA NETWORKER

Since you won't get clients (or cash) if you're hiding out behind your computer—shocker!—you *need* to get out there and network.

I'm sure you've got this by now. But did you know that there's actually a right way (and a wrong way) to network?

Networking is so important that I actually spend a whole session going over networking strategies with my Concierge Academy students! We've also spent a bit of time on it in this book, but we'll go deeper in this chapter, because ninja networking is *absolutely* the best and fastest way to grow a concierge business.

In addition to showing up at the right places (read: the places where your ideal clients will be), you'll need to know a few things to get the most out of your networking experiences and get your business on the fast track. So here are my Ninja Networking Do's and Don'ts!

NINJA NETWORKING
DO'S AND DON'TS

- DO show up with business cards. Seriously. Bring about fifty more than you think you'll need. There's nothing worse than wrapping up a promising conversation only to find yourself sans cards. It looks unprofessional, and it might cost you a relationship. So, right now, put a stack of cards in every bag you own, a few more in your wallet, and a spare box in your car! You should also bring business cards to the gym, the grocery store, the mall, your neighbor's kid's birthday party … anywhere you might meet an ideal client. You never know who you might run into!

- DO identify at least 3 groups where you will meet ideal clients and COIs. If your target is high-wealth individuals, you need to be where they are, or be networking with centers of influence and referral partners who know them.

- DO commit to at least one group for 6 months. Showing up at events every once in a while doesn't help you build relationships quickly.
So identify a group you like, and make a commitment to attend every meeting for six straight months. Put the dates on your calendar

right now, and don't break them for anything short of a real emergency.

- DON'T join groups that you don't enjoy or won't go to consistently. Even if some of your ideal clients might be there, don't waste your time at events where you don't like the people or can't be yourself. Also, don't commit to groups that require a crazy commute or take place at odd hours. You'll be less likely to attend, and your networking will be less effective.

- DON'T shove business cards in everyone's faces. Networking is all about building relationships, and those relationships need to be genuine in order to thrive. Instead of butterflying around the room, talk to three or four people whose businesses and ideas genuinely interest you, and who actually seem interested in you. If there are more people you want to connect with, save it for the next event, or get their cards at the end of the night and say, "I know we didn't get a chance to chat tonight, but I would love to talk to you more. Would it be okay if I e-mailed you to set up a coffee date?"

And, most importantly of all ...

- DON'T forget to follow up! Th s is the most important step in creating relationships! A short note to say, "It was great to meet you yesterday!I'd love to learn more about you and what you do," is often enough to start a conversation.

By networking, you are making yourself visible. You're putting a face to your name, making connections, and nurturing relationships. A concierge can't ask for more!

WHERE *to* SPEND YOUR MARKETING DOLLARS

This is a big hurdle for many new concierge business owners, and second only to the question of how to market as a cause of confusion and stress.

In order to market successfully, you have to have an idea of where to spend not only your marketing dollars, but also your personal time and energy.

Last week I had a call with someone who really, *really* wanted to come to a live event I was hosting. "I know it's something I need," she told me, "and I know I'll learn a lot, but I just can't."

When I asked her why she couldn't come, her response was, "I just spent a bunch of money to run an ad in a local paper."

I'll be honest: my heart kinda broke.

The reality is, a one-shot deal in the local paper will very rarely net you any long-term clients. The statistics don't lie: all marketing *must* be done on a consistent basis. Again, the magic is in the follow-up: it's all about consistency.

Not all marketing is good marketing. As you look at the Marketing Wheel and decide how you're going to address each spoke, think about what methods will have the biggest return on investment (ROI) and potential for long-term growth. (Hint: they're *not* the one-time ads!)

So, my friend who owns a concierge business spent all her money on a one time shot at success, instead of investing her money in long term growth. And how many clients do you think she got from that ad?

You guessed it: None. Zero.

Don't be that person. Spend your marketing money where it counts!

3 SMART WAYS TO USE YOUR MARKETING DOLLARS

1. Networking

2. Getting to know people (aka, building relationships)

3. Investing in yourself

Smart Marketing Investment #1: Networking

Yup, here we are again. By this point, you're probably sick of reading about networking.

Too bad.

As your business grows and you start to get more clients, you will create a referral network that is a bit more self-sustaining—but in the beginning, you've got to get your butt out there and talk to people, and that takes resources.

I was presenting at a business bootcamp a few months back, and met a woman who does social media for small businesses. I asked where she was networking. I asked her how her business was going.

Her response: "Nobody wants to pay for my services."

I'd heard that one before—out of my own mouth, when I was still struggling to launch my business. Immediately, I knew the solution.

"Where are you networking?" I asked.

"Online, mostly. I go to a few meetups, too. "

"What about joining your local chamber of commerce, or a local business group that meets weekly?"

"I can't afford that," she said.

"Really? Not even $25 for an after-work party?"

"I really can't."

I decided to be frank. "Maybe you should consider that people who pay to invest in their networking are also more willing to invest in services and products—like yours—that help them grow their businesses. Do you think they might be a better target audience for your services? I mean, you've got to put your money where the clients are."

She stood there, baffled, as I said goodbye and walked away.

The lesson: free events attract people who like free stuff.

Smart Marketing Investment #2: Getting to know people (aka, building relationships)

Here's where most people slack off. Once they do their networking, they think they're going to do business with their new contacts right away.

Wrong. Most business doesn't happen that way. Most business happens *after* the networking events. I call this "secondary networking."

Whether the people you meet at these events eventually become clients or not, chances are they know a lot of people. And even if they don't need your services right now, the people in their network might.

Imagine that every person you meet knows just 100 people. (Most know far more.) If you get to know ten people a month, and each of those ten people likes and trusts you enough to refer clients, you are in essence actively networking to 1,000 people a month! Mind-blowing, right?

But here's the thing: if those ten initial contacts don't get the chance to know, like, and trust you, they won't refer the people in their network to you. So you need to invest in the follow-up—whether you think your contact will become a customer or not.

Here are four easy ways to invest in getting to know people.

1. Coffee dates (in-person or virtual)
2. Sending letters/cards
3. Sending thank you notes
4. Creating follow-up systems

Even if you're not sure there will be a payoff, take the time to get to know the people you connect with. You never know who they know!

Smart Marketing Investment #3: Investing in yourself

Besides being the person you spend the most time with, you are the core of your business—the one asset the business simply cannot do without.

Investing in yourself is never a risk, and it always pays off. Even seemingly "bad" investments (like my first couple of business coaches) are still worthwhile, because you always learn *something*. And, when you take a risk, you push yourself beyond your comfort zone and into a new set of experiences. Every time you do this is practice for the next time—which could be the time when it really matters.

My two favorite ways to invest in myself are education and my health.

As Tony Robbins says, "The Key to Success? Model the Best!"

Education doesn't stop when you graduate from college. Learning new stuff keeps your mind fresh and your skills relevant. Once you learn something, you can never unlearn it. So, take a class, go to a workshop, or dive into a hands-on learning experience. The growth you'll see in yourself is worth every penny. You won't regret it.

Health is the other area I prioritize. During my career as a nurse, I saw a lot of people who were suffering because they simply didn't take care of their bodies. Once I started my business, I saw another side to things: keeping myself healthy was the best way to ensure that my business stayed healthy, too. After all, I can't be productive and serve my clients if I'm sick, tired, or in pain.

So, even if you don't feel like you have the cash right now, invest in a gym membership, or at least a good pair of walking/running shoes. Add a green smoothie to your day. Buy healthy food instead of convenience food. Small, simple things will add up fast. (Plus, you never know who might need your services at the gym. Wink, wink!)

WHAT *to* DO WHEN *the* PHONE RINGS

So, you've gotten out there. You've networked like a ninja. You've followed up with your new contacts and identified your COIs. You've been smart with your marketing dollars. You've followed all of my advice and taken the fast route to cash, and now you're dancing on your tiptoes, waiting to see the results.

Then, finally, the moment you've been waiting for: the phone rings.

This is one of the most exciting moments of your Concierge Life. It can also be one of the most petrifying.

You are about to take what's called a "sales call." Meaning, you will be sharing with the person on the other end of the line what you can do to help them, and how much you will charge.

I used to freeze up during sales calls. I would stutter, and mumble, and pretty much apologize for existing and wanting to charge actual money for what I offered. Thankfully, I got over it—and you will too.

Here are 5 tips to help you have successful sales conversations and get that cash fl wing into your bank account!

Sales Call Strategy #1: Always respond to calls within 24 hours

Duh, right? Well, no. Sometimes, we get busy or scared, and we drop the ball—and lose the client. So make callbacks a priority.

In general, when people decide to take the leap and call you for help, they need that help, like, yesterday. So don't procrastinate! Get back to people as soon as you reasonably can.

That said, don't take sales calls from the car, your kid's soccer game, or while you're sitting on the toilet. (I'm not kidding! People do this!) Wait until you can be back at your desk, and you won't be interrupted mid-convo by beeping horns, screaming fans, or (gross!) the flush.

Sales Call Strategy #2: Don't let them catch you off-guard!

Imagine this: I'm driving home from a two-hour networking gig, after already working for six hours with a client during the day, going grocery shopping, and picking up my husband's dry cleaning. I'm tired, I have to pee, and my kiddos are waiting for me at the door. Honestly, I'm a little cranky!

I'm finally pulling into my driveway when my cell phone rings. It's someone who's interested in our services.

When I first started, I would have picked up that phone right there in the driveway. I would have forced myself to have that sales conversation with my bladder about to burst and the kids staring at me with arms crossed, wondering when I was coming inside. And it would have sucked.

Now, I know better. If you aren't in a good place to talk to a client, don't pick up the phone. You're much better off calling them back in fifteen minutes, or even an hour, when you're more settled, focused, and prepared for the conversation. No good conversations happen on a full bladder—just sayin'!

Sales Call Strategy #3: Prepare for your calls

If possible, connect with your prospects via e-mail before scheduled calls. Th s allows you to send any necessary information to them beforehand, and give you a sense of what they need and why they want to work with you.

Th s may sound silly, but take the time to get into the right mindset before your call. Remember, you are the expert and your services can literally save their life! So do your deep breathing, light a candle, take a short walk—whatever it takes to put you in a good place to have a productive sales convo.

Sales Call Strategy #4: Be ready to explain how you work

Too many times, people forget to explain their process. Your clients want to know how you work, how you charge, and what the process "looks like." You can alleviate their fears and concerns by conveying your process to them in a clear manner from start to fin sh, with a focus on ease of use (meaning, they don't have to do a bunch of work to work with you). Examples of how you've worked with previous clients are also helpful.

Sales Call Strategy #5: Demonstrate your competency

Many a sales conversation goes awry when you cannot convey confidence and competency in what you do. Be sure you are prepared to converse about what your prospect is trying to accomplish, what's preventing them from accomplishing it, and how you can help them achieve their goals. When you have confidence in what you do, your clients will, too!

* * * * *

All of the work you've done to put yourself on the fast track to cash will be for nothing if you can't close the sale when people call. So do what you need to do to get comfortable with talking about what you do, how you do it, and what you charge for it. Practice on your spouse or your friends. Talk to yourself in front of the mirror or while you're driving. Write out your sales pitch and practice them over and over, like a speech. Read your marketing copy aloud to yourself with feeling and excitement. Whatever it takes to make your sales calls feel natural and automatic—and your potential clients feel confident and excited to work with you!

The BIG LESSON

The fastest path to cash isn't a shortcut. (If you were hoping for that, sorry to disappoint you; it doesn't exist, no matter what the marketing "gurus" say!) Instead, it's a direct route to cultivating and nurturing the kinds of profitable relationships that are the heart of any successful Concierge Life.

And let's face it, the relationships are what you're really in this for, anyway.

So get out there, my friend. Connect. Nurture. Be who you are, and let your desire to help people take center stage. You *can* do this.

Chapter 8

MOVIN' ON UP

WHEW! YOU DID IT! You made it to the end of the book (well, almost). I'm giving you a virtual hi-five right now!

If you're anything like me, this book is already dog-eared, highlighted, and plastered with mini Post-its. And, if you're a total freak like me, those Post-its are color-coded.

You've learned my secrets to creating a successful Concierge Life, and the marketing tools and techniques that have made my business totally kick-ass. But, my friend (and we are friends now, right?), the work doesn't end here. In fact, it's only beginning.

Now, you need to take everything you've learned in this book—all the notes you took, all the advice you highlighted —and put it to use in the real world.

See, there's one more thing that can make or break your concierge business that we haven't discussed yet ... and that's ignoring good advice.

Please don't let this book become just another "shelf-help" dust magnet. I wrote this for *you*—to help you get started, and succeed where others have failed—because, guess what? I need you. I need my peeps out there, all across the world, to stand up, shine your lights, live your passion, and help me change the world, one service at a time. I can't do it alone.

(I actually cried while writing the line above, which is how I know it's my truth. I told you, way back at the beginning of this book, about my belief about concierges: that if this is really your truth, and your path, you are one of the chosen few who are here to take care of others in our world. So don't let me down, okay?)

Now, before you head back into the trenches and start putting this book to real-world use, I want to make sure you're prepared. Not prepared to do the work—I know you're good on that front—but prepared to stay committed through thick and thin, and through all the good, bad, and scary places that can happen when you're starting a business and things don't go exactly as planned.

With that in mind, I want to share five more pieces of advice to carry you through the next stage of your growth. These things will likely come up—they do for almost everyone—but if you surround yourself with the right peeps, and do what it takes to keep your mindset in check, you *will* end up creating your very own awesome-sauce Concierge Life. Even more, you'll do your part to change the world by doing what you love most.

Let these five things become your mantras. Repeat them to yourself in front of the mirror when you feel insecure. Post them on your wall. Let them carry you through the tough days, and the bum weeks. Remember that everything you want is possible—as long as you persevere.

Concierge Mantra #1: "Give it time"

Things *will* take longer than you expect. It's just a fact of the Concierge Life.

It may take you three months of consistent marketing to land your first big client. Or it may take you six months, or even nine months. Be prepared, and be patient. They will come.

There is no secret sauce, and there are no shortcuts to success. You have to take the journey, and experience the evolution of you that happens along the way. Sometimes it sucks to wait it out—but in the end, I promise it will be worth it.

So, if you tried something once (like that local networking group or following up with a potential client by e-mail) and didn't get the results you expected, don't give up. Just because nothing is happening yet doesn't mean that nothing will happen. Just keep doing what you do, and let what you've put out there come back to you in its own time.

Also, don't ever, ever compare your journey to someone else's. Mom and Grandma probably told you this when you were a kid, but it's even more important now that you're in the business world. Everyone has a different path to success, and different setbacks. So stop trying to "measure up," and stop judging yourself.

Concierge Mantra #2: "Don't listen to the naysayers"

People who put you down have *no idea* what you're capable of. So don't listen to them. They don't know jack.

Surround yourself with the right people—the ones who will love and support you no matter what. As your entrepreneurial journey continues, you'll gain confidence. Once you have a few big successes behind you, you'll be unstoppable.

If you're the type who loves a challenge, use those naysayers' words as fuel for your rocket ship. Thank them for their input, and then say to yourself, "Oh, yeah? Watch this, buddy!" And launch.

If you're super-sensitive, like me, don't let those negative words in at all. Just tune them out, do something that makes you feel good (like the mindset practices I shared in Chapter 4), and get the hell on with it.

No matter what others say, believe in your own possibilities.

Concierge Mantra #3: "It's okay to make mistakes"

As a recovering perfectionist, this one has taken me *years* to unravel. What I've learned is that there is a difference between wanting to make sure things are as flawless as possible in your work, and hiding out because you're scared to mess up.

As I shared earlier in this book, there are no real mistakes. Our "errors" are just opportunities to improve ourselves, so we can pivot, refine our strategies, and do our best work here on Earth.

So, keep on making those mistakes. Just don't miss the opportunity to learn from them.

Concierge Mantra #4: "Follow your heart, no matter what"

If I had listened to my head, you would not be holding this book in your hands right now.

My head told me, "You're not a writer. What the hell do you know about books?" My heart said, "Let it unfold."

Thank God my head is not the driving force behind my purpose, or my Concierge Life.

I know I'm not the only person in the world who fi hts those nagging voices in my head. The difference between me and so many other people is that I've learned to beat them at their own game. Instead of asking my head, "What's the problem," I ask my heart, "What's the solution?" Then, once my heart answers, my head (which is pretty smart, when it behaves) can get on board.

No matter what your head says, you are good enough. You are smart and talented enough. And most importantly, what you do *matters*.

Your heart, your soul, the deep place inside you where you know the truth… this is where your most important decisions should be made. Always choose what leads you into happiness, joy, and fulfillment, and not what leads you into guilt, stress, or resentment. Let your heart lead—even if it means letting go of that obnoxious client who keeps you up at night, or discontinuing a package that doesn't adequately compensate you for your time and effort.

When it gets tough, remember that your heart can always see where you're going, even if your head can't. Learn to trust what you know, deep inside, and do whatever's necessary to get your brain on board.

Concierge Mantra #5: "Give it your all"

"Did I truly give it my all?"

This is the question that separates the dabblers from the masters. On a scale of one to ten, are you *really* rockin' it? Or have you really been knocking around at a four or five?

Only you can answer that question. So answer it honestly. All the goodness happens when we're focused and consistent in our marketing, our message, and our energy. So ... are you showing up all-in at your networking groups? Are you following up and implementing those KIT campaigns with enthusiasm? Are you excited for each and every sales call? Are you putting your whole heart and soul into your business, regardless of how scary it feels?

If not, I understand. Being all-in is intense. But if you want to succeed—really succeed—you've got to turn up the volume. So pick one marketing strategy that you're already doing, and amp it up to a ten. You'll be amazed at what happens.

The BIG LESSON

In this book, I've given you all of the tools I can to help you embark upon your Concierge Life journey. You have a strong foundation that you can build on with confide ce. The next steps are up to you.

Be brave. Be strong. And stay committed. You are here to help others—and the best way for you to do that is to build a thriving business that touches as many lives as possible. Your heart is calling you to be successful. So tap into that passion and purpose, do what you've got to do to get over the humps, and keep movin' on.

Th s book is your kick in the pants—the permission you need to get out there and start Getting Shit Done. So go forth, friend, and get ready to fly.

With love,

PS: A book is the best way for me to give you these basics—but it's not as personalized. as a conversation. So, if you're looking for real-life solutions and information for your unique business, I'd love to invite you to join my Concierge Academy. You can learn more and book an exploratory call with me at TheConciergeAcademy.com.

Bonus

KELLY'S TOOLBOX

YOU'RE READY TO STOP messing around, and start creating your Concierge Life. Awesome-sauce!

You were born to help other people. You know it, I know it. I believe in you and what you're doing.

That's why, as a gift to you, I'm including three of the most powerful worksheets and assessments I use with my Concierge Academy students in this bonus section. These will help you put the theory you've learned in the last hundred pages into practice. They're like fuel for your rocket ship!

Are you ready? Then let's turn the page and get started!

The CONCIERGE ACADEMY™
MARKETING WHEEL

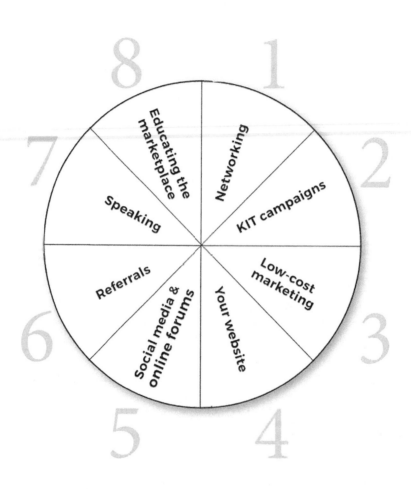

ACTION STEP

In the space below, write all of the specific tools and activities
you plan to use to work with your Marketing Wheel.

1. Networking _____

_____

2. KIT campaigns _____

_____

3. Low-cost marketing _____

_____

4. Your Website _____

_____

5. Social media _____

_____

6. Referrals _____

_____

7. Speaking _____

_____

8. Educating the marketplace _____

_____

The CONCIERGE ACADEMY™ BUSINESS VISION *and* COMMITMENT ASSESSMENT

In order to make improvements in your business, you have to be aware of where you currently are!

After working through this assessment, you'll be able to concretely identify areas in your business where you can take action!

Awareness is the first step. Next up: implementation!
To begin you need a concrete vision! This will morph and change as you grow, so just go with your vision as you see it right now. What do you want your business to look like? What are your big dreams for your Concierge Life?

Use the space on the next page to write down the current vision you have for your business. In your vision statement, be sure to include information like:

- How many clients do you want to serve?
- What demographics do you wish to work with?
- Do you want to expand your location?
- Do you want to have a team or be a solopreneur?

There is no wrong answer—and the only right answer is *your* answer!

ACTION STEP #1

MY VISION *for* MY CONCIERGE LIFE

_____

_____

_____

_____

_____

_____

_____

_____

_____

_____

_____

_____

_____

_____

_____

_____

_____

_____

_____

_____

_____

ACTION STEP #2
KNOWLEDGE *and* COMMITMENT TEST

On a scale of 1 to 10, grade yourself on your current knowledge and commitment level to your business and marketing. Be truthful with yourself. No one has to see this but you.

Once the awareness is there, you can take action and actually *measure* the improvement you have made!

_____ 1. Looking at where I want to go, how committed have I been to my vision?

_____ 2. I am confide t with my business as it is right now.

_____ 3. I have a current marketing calendar that I am living by: ___ Daily ___Weekly ___Monthly ___Quarterly

_____ 4. How committed have I been in my marketing?

_____ 5. I am doing everything I can to grow my business right now.

_____ 6. I am networking effectively *and* getting results.

_____ 7. I stay in touch with all prospects in a kind, gentle way.

_____ 8. When I have sales conversations, I feel confide t stating my rates and conveying the value my services provide.

_____ 9. I have done everything I can to be fully committed to grow my business and meet my vision.

Anything less than a 10 leaves room for improvement!

This isn't about being "perfect," but rather recognizing where you can improve to reach the vision you hold deep within your heart.

* * * * *

Use the space below to reflect. What will it feel like for you to see your vision come true? How will it affect your life? Your finances? Your future? What will it feel like to live as your "future self"?

_____

_____

_____

_____

_____

_____

_____

_____

_____

_____

_____

_____

_____

_____

_____

The CONCIERGE ACADEMY™
IDEAL CLIENT PROFILE
WORKSHEET

Describe the type of client you would prefer to work with

(personality): _____

_____

_____

What is the age range of your ideal clients? _____ to _____

What is the gender of your ideal clients? __M   __F   __N/A

Where are your ideal clients likely to live?

_____Urban   _____Suburban   _____Rural   _____Other

Geographic location? _____

What are the most likely occupations of your potential clients?

_____

_____

_____

_____

What does a typical client want from the services you are
providing? _____

_____

_____

_____

_____

_____

What makes your services stand out from local competition?
(Also known as Unique Selling Proposition or USP)

_____

_____

_____

_____

What factors or emotional changes have to occur for your
ideal clients before they will engage your services?

_____

_____

_____

_____

What do your ideal clients need most right now? _____

_____

_____

_____

_____

_____

_____

_____

Does your ideal client have the financial stability to engage in

your services? _____

_____

_____

_____

_____

_____

Sneak Peek

THE CONCIERGE ACADEMY™

IN THE CONCIERGE ACADEMY™, we spend a lot of time working in depth on the things we covered in this book, like marketing, mindset, and networking strategies. We also do a lot of "homework"—but not the boring, headache-inducing homework you're used to. We use action steps to shake things up and get you thinking!

The following are a few of the fun activities and assessments I ask my students to do during our time together. I'm sharing them to give you a sneak peek into the nurturing world of the Academy, and get you thinking about your business in a whole new way!

YOUR ELEVATOR SPEECH

This week I want you to work on your elevator speech.

When you're crafting your elevator speech, the idea is really to just engage someone's curiosity. That's it—nothing else!

It's called an "elevator speech" because it describes a challenge: How would you explain your business and make a sale if fate placed you in an elevator with your dream prospect, and you only had sixty seconds to make your pitch before the doors opened, and your prospect walked away?

You want to say something that feels comfortable to you. Then test it and tweak it until it flows consistently and naturally.

How to craft a memorable elevator speech

To put a good pitch together, you'll want to ask yourself a few questions:

- How do I work with clients?
- What value do I/we provide?
- How do we provide this value?
- What makes us unique?
- Who is my target market?

How do you become more comfortable? Use it, say it, and practice it! You can practice by yourself in front of a mirror, try it out on your spouse, or call your best friend.

You can also test your elevator speech at your next roundtable-type networking group! I have often heard people stand up and say, "I wrote a new thirty-second commercial. Can I use that today and get some feedback?"

If you don't feel truly confide t with your elevator pitch, take time this week to rewrite it and practice it; then, get back out there and use it until it simply flows out of you!

One note: as you grow, your business grows, and you truly hone in on your ideal clients, your elevator speech will change —and that's totally okay! Don't try to get it "perfect." Just get excited about it right now!

* * * * *

MAXIMIZE YOUR CLIENT EXPERIENCE

One of the greatest ways to build lifelong clients is through an exceptional client experience. People come to you when they have a problem, but they stay with you because they love the experience you provide.

Not only does an amazing client experience keep your clients with you longer, but it brings clients back even if they only use you "once in a while". And, anyone who feels amazing when using your service is more likely to refer new clients to you!

Here's an example of how we at Task Complete create a great client experience.

When we house-sit for a client we always leave behind a "welcome home" card. If we are caring for their gardens, we often cut three flowers and leave them in the kitchen so the client will see them as they enter. These two simple things let our clients know they are appreciated and that we care.

When crafting your client experiences, allow your creativity to shine through! Do you love ice cream? Invite your clients and COIs to a Client Appreciation ice cream social. (See how you can do the two-birds-with-one-stone thing there?)

Do you love music? Make an old-fashioned "mix tape" (on a CD, of course) and share it with your clients.

The idea is to infuse more of your personality into your business while simultaneously creating an experience that your clients will *never* get anywhere else!

What are 5 ways you can enhance your clients' experience?

1. _____

2. _____

3. _____

4. _____

5. _____

* * * * *

CLEAN UP YOUR WORK SPACE

Working in a cluttered, disorganized space can be distracting, and cause you to lose focus! Loss of focus negatively impacts your productivity and therefore your income!

I have also learned that when we are in a cluttered space we create clogged "energy" around us.

So, put aside at least an hour this week and start purging! By cleaning and clearing out, you open the fl w of energy into your office. Whenever I purge and clean my office, it always brings in new clients because I'm opening up space around me!

Cleaning and clearing tips

Be sure to …

1. Clear the top of your desk.

2. Purge old papers and handouts you'll never use again.

3. Clean out the filing cabinet and make room for new clients.

4. Purge anything that no longer serves you or a purpose.

5. Be sure your floor is clear!

6. Open the windows.

7. Burn sage, incense, or a candle while you're clearing.

SEE ALL THAT YOU DO!

Sometimes, as entrepreneurs, we move so fast and do so many different things that we tend to not notice how much we've accomplished!

The downside to this is that, when we don't acknowledge our accomplishments and successes on a regular basis, we have the false assumption that we're not actually getting much done or that we aren't making much progress! (Sound familiar?)

We are often our biggest critics—but being hard on ourselves doesn't help us succeed. Self-criticism affects our self-confidence, and when our confidence is negatively impacted, we take far less action.

So, right now, take a moment to look back at what you accomplished over the last week. Then, list ten successes you experienced, or things you are grateful to have worked on. These can be anything from "I met five new people while networking" to "I received one new referral."

For bonus points, start a separate "gratitude journal" that you write in each and every day. Sometimes it's hard to stay motivated, but being present to all that you have already done will inspire you and fuel you to do more!

My successes this week

1. _____

2. _____

3. _____

4. _____

5. _____

6. _____

7. _____

8. _____

9. _____

10. _____

* * * * *

BETTER SERVE THE CLIENTS YOU ALREADY HAVE

You absolutely *must* stay on top of the needs of your clients!

Building a relationship with your clients allows them to open up to you as well. Th s means you can obtain critical information that you can then use to help support them even more.

For example: If you know they're getting ready to travel, support them that way. If they have a party coming up, offer to help prep/plan and be on hand for the party. If you know their parents are aging or ill, and you work with seniors, remind them of that, too.

How do you get to know these details about your clients? You have to *ask them*!

This week, call your clients and ask them for fifteen minutes of their time. (I highly recommend offering them one free hour of service as compensation, because one thing our clients always want/need is more time!)

Before you get on the phone, prepare a list of five to ten questions you want to ask. Be very deliberate in what you ask, because their time is highly valuable and you may never get them on the phone again!

Questions I want to ask my clients

1. _____

2. _____

3. _____

4. _____

5. _____

6. _____

7. _____

8. _____

9. _____

10. _____

The Concierge Academy™

Are you ready to make money helping others?

Join us in our Fully Booked Business Club where you will discover:

- How to stand out in the marketplace
- Easy, creative, and affordable ways to market your services (hint: they're not what you think!)
- Who to network with and why
- How to utilize social media without wasting your time
- How to price and package your services
- How to create an effective website
- How to stay focused and consistent with your marketing

This 6-month, high-volume program is made up of 6 modules, delivered audio and PowerPoint downloads, worksheets, and other resources. You'll also have access to monthly group Q&A calls where you can submit your questions ahead of time to Kelly!

Learn more and register today at
yourconciergeacademy.com/fb-biz-club

Connect with Kelly

Learn more about The Concierge Academy™
and read Kelly's blog at
TheConciergeAcademy.com

Social Media

Facebook
Facebook.com/TheKellySchaefer

LinkedIn
LinkedIn.com/in/KellyannSchaefer

Instagram
instagram.com/thekellyschaefer/

YouTube
youtube.com/c/TheConciergeAcademy/videos

Acknowledgments

WITH LOVE AND GRATITUDE

I WOULD LIKE TO THANK my husband and four children, for providing me with unconditional love and support. Without you, this entrepreneurial journey would not be possible. I am a million times blessed to live this life and journey with each of you by my side. Each and every day, you remind me how much I love my life and the people in it, and that it's my mission in life to bring love into this world. Thank you for holding me up when I want to fall done, giving me hugs when I feel sad or alone, and for believing in me when I can't do so myself.

My husband, you are always my rock; thank you for

being the place from which I draw much of my strength, and for your humor, which always makes things lighter. My greatest success in life is having you each by my side. Thank you for refl cting to me how to be self-forgiving, patient, full of wonder, and never too serious. You are my muse for creating and living a better life, and enjoying every moment of blessing we have. Time and time again you have allowed me to follow my heart and my passion to the dreams I have been called to discover, for we each came to this life with gifts hat are meant to change the world.

To my team: thank you following me on this crazy journey, and for believing in our mission to positively impact a million lives. It is through your love, devotion, and commitment to service that we have a greater reach in the world. None of this would be possible without you.

To our concierge clients: thank you for allowing us to use our gifts of love and compassion to take care of you; it's for you that we get up every day and do this work. Thank you even more for teaching me that I, too, deserve to receive love, kindness, and time for self-care and emotional freedom.

SPECIAL SHOUT-OUTS

To Katharine Giovanni, whom I consider the mother of our industry: without your bravery and commitment to us, the personal concierges of the world, we would have had no path to follow. Thank you for leading the way.

To my good friend Leslie Spoor: thank you for always picking up the phone in those moments when I want to quit. You remind me to stay the course, and to let my heart, my belief, and my positive expectations pull me forward.

To my assistant *extraordinaire* Jill: You were a hand from God given directly to me at the exact right moment—and more importantly for being my "string." I hope to enrich your world as much as your kindness, love, understanding and compassion enrich mine. Love, your Pooh Bear.

To my friend Stacey Martino: thank you for always being willing to "hold the bucket" when I feel overwhelmed. You have helped keep my family alive in so many ways.

To my editor Bryna Haynes, and her team: first off, how cool is it that I get to have an editor! Thank you for helping me stay the course, to not give in when things got hard, and for helping me share not just my words but my truth with the world, so that others can find solace in my words when they feel lost or alone.

To Brenda Jankowski, my photographer: you captured the pure essence of everything I had envisioned this book cover would look like. And, most importantly, you helped me feel confident in my own skin. I will forever remember the moment you took that photo, and the moment I felt the tears of "this is it" well up in my eyes!

AND, FINALLY ...

To *you*, the reader of this book!

I dedicate this to you, and your bravery to follow your heart and be of service to others. When you shine your light, we have a collective chance of overshadowing the darkness that tries to cripple our world. Together, we will leave behind a legacy of love, service, and compassion.

About the Author

KELLYANN SCHAEFER

KELLYANN SCHAEFER is an entrepreneur, three-time international best-selling author, and the CEO and Founder of TaskComplete.Com, an award-winning personal concierge company. She is uniquely skilled at assisting her clients and fellow entrepreneurs to make more money, create more time, and increase their impact on the world.

As a mom of four and Registered Nurse, Kelly knows all too well how difficult it can be to balance a home while also building a successful heart-centered business. Her business is built on the core value of building relationships; this helps her to anticipate the needs of her clients on multiple levels.

In 2014, Kelly began supporting and coaching other concierge companies through her Concierge Academy, with the goal of helping others in her industry reach more clients and grow profitable concierge businesses while becoming industry leaders and living the ultimate Concierge Life.

When she's not plotting her takeover of the concierge world, Kelly focuses her time and energy on three initiatives that are near and dear to her heart and mission: ending hunger, supporting abused and downtrodden women, and helping sick children find solace in the arms of stuffed pandas through "Operation Panda Healing."

Learn more about Kelly at TheConciergeAcademy.com.

Made in the USA
Middletown, DE
01 August 2021